The Moment

THE MOMENT

*Changemakers on
Why and How They Joined
the Fight for Social Justice*

STEVE FIFFER

NEWSOUTH BOOKS
an imprint of
The University of Georgia Press
Athens

NSB

Published by NewSouth Books
an imprint of the University of Georgia Press
Athens, Georgia 30602
www.ugapress.org/imprints.newsouthbooks/

The paper in this book meets the guidelines for permanence and
durability of the Committee on Production Guidelines for Book
Longevity of the Council on Library Resources.

Most NewSouth/University of Georgia Press titles
are available from popular ebook vendors.

Printed in Canada
22 23 24 25 26 P 5 4 3 2 1

Library of Congress Control Number: 2022944344

ISBN 9781588384751 (paperback : alk. paper)
ISBN 9781588384850 (ebook)

To Sharon, for all the moments

To read the stories of other
changemakers who are not in
the book, to share the story of your
own moment, and to view discussion questions for classrooms,
book groups, and workshops,
please visit our website:
themoment-thebook.com.

Contents

Preface

I can come pretty close to pinpointing the moment I had the idea for this book. It came shortly after the March 2021 publication by NewSouth Books of *It's in the Action: Memories of a Nonviolent Warrior*, the posthumous memoir of civil rights icon Dr. C. T. Vivian. I'd had the privilege of collaborating on the book, and in the course of my involvement had become good friends with one of Dr. Vivian's daughters, Denise Morse.

The light bulb went off after Denise sent me a copy of a sermon her father had given. Dr. Vivian, whom Martin Luther King Jr. once called "the greatest preacher ever to live," had typed the text. But on several pages of the sermon, he had handwritten his mantra, "It's in the action." The good doctor had wanted to remind himself to stress to his audience that justice and equality will never be achieved if all we do is wring our hands or complain. We must act.

In July, I acted, sending a memo to my publisher Suzanne La Rosa that read in part:

> I would interview people—well known and little known, of all ages, races, and backgrounds—and record their stories of the moment they realized, as C. T. always said, "It's in the action" and became involved in the social justice movement. . . .
>
> I'm interested in learning and conveying: What specific event/experience or series of events/experiences moved these individuals to get involved in social justice activism? So, in these interviews I'd ask, among other things, what their life was like before they got involved; what moved them to take action; how they weighed the decision to act—pros and cons; what form their action took; what

the experience is/was like; how it impacted and changed them and others; what advice they'd give to others who have yet to act/ may be considering acting.

Suzanne was enthusiastic, and thus began one of the most enlightening and fulfilling journeys of my life.

I will be forever grateful to the changemakers whose words follow for their thoughtful, candid, and, often, poignant responses—not to mention their own efforts. Those responses were as varied as the changemakers themselves, but there was one theme that arose over and over again: the importance of storytelling.

Telling one's own story can be healing to the storyteller in addition to moving an audience to act or legislate. And it can certainly open the listener's eyes. This particular listener, for example, never gave enough thought to how important it was for black parents to give their children black dolls or Santas that couldn't be found in stores and to expose them to books by or about African Americans that couldn't be found in schools. I didn't fully understand the psychological damage that appropriated team mascots can inflict on indigenous people, particularly children. And I never gave much thought to how much architecture and design can result in injustice and inequality. I promise that your eyes, too, will be opened, thanks to these stories.

The interviews for this book were conducted during a less than sunny period. The nation was in the middle of the Covid crisis and still dealing with effects of the January 6 insurrection, the murder of George Floyd (and others). Congress was unable to pass criminal justice reform legislation or a voting rights bill to preempt actual election steals plotted by undemocratic state legislators. Local school boards were banning books. Even the baseball season was delayed.

What a saving grace it was to speak with every person whose story follows. To a professional basketball player who took the season off to work for social justice. To a CEO insisting his company have a "heart and soul" and commit to help revive a troubled city. To students creating projects and platforms to fight injustice. To teachers trying to tell the true story of historical events. Reading about the indignities and obstacles so many on these pages faced, you might marvel, as I do, that they all have the energy, desire and optimism to fight for social justice instead of just throw up their hands. But they all have put those hands to wonderful work. I dare you not to be inspired . . . and to act when your own moment arrives.

I also invite you to visit the website: themoment-thebook.com. There you will see the stories of other changemakers, past and present, not in the book. Many of these stories will be written by students who will be using *The Moment* in their classrooms. And we hope that you will consider sharing on the website stories of your own moment or of others whom you admire.

Acknowledgments

I'm forever grateful to the changemakers featured on these pages for the work they do and their kindness in finding time to share their stories with me.

Once those stories had been shared, a remarkable group of people helped me turn them into a book. Thanks first and foremost to my friends at NewSouth Books—visionary publisher Suzanne La Rosa, editor extraordinaire Randall Williams, and team members Beth Marino, Lisa Emerson, Lisa Harrison, Kelly Snyder, and Sarah Williams, indexers Anna Grace Graham and McCormick Williams, and cover designer Laura Murray.

The University of Georgia Press, which wisely acquired NewSouth earlier this year, has also been extremely helpful. I extend my thanks to their team.

Others, too, were essential to the process. My best reader, editor, and calming influence: my incredible wife Sharon. Dear friends and sounding boards: Lisa Sablosky and Howard Rossman. Inspirations: the late C. T. Vivian and his daughter Denise Morse. And talented website designer: Chris Bomm.

Thanks, too, to Susie Bright, Paul Guarino, Mariel Edokwe, Mahalah Lewis, Caitlin McCaskey, Minjae Park, Margie Schaps, Elodie Mailliet Storm, Stacie Marshall, Amy Donofrio, Malcolm Jones, and the indomitable Gail Hochman.

The Moment

How wonderful it is that nobody need wait a single moment before starting to improve the world.

—ANNE FRANK

Every moment is an organizing opportunity, every person a potential activist, every minute a chance to change the world.

—DOLORES HUERTA

'To Help Condemned People'

BRYAN STEVENSON, *62, is the founder and executive director of the Equal Justice Initiative, a human rights organization in Montgomery, Alabama. A graduate of Harvard Law School, Stevenson also led the creation of two acclaimed cultural sites: the Legacy Museum and the National Memorial for Peace and Justice. He is a MacArthur Fellow and has been recognized by* Time *as one of "The 100 Most Influential People." The 2019 movie,* Just Mercy, *was based on his best-selling 2014 memoir of the same name.*

WHEN MY BROTHER WENT to the integrated school in Milton, Delaware, a year before the rest of the black kids came, it was a voluntary integration period. During lunch, he and a Latino boy would get chased by all of the white kids. So my mother would take me to the school at lunchtime, and she would let me get on the car and climb over the fence. My brother would then run to this spot on the playground and we would, you know, tussle with these kids. My mom basically said, "You're gonna go help your brother." I was like four or five years old, and it didn't feel like fighting; it almost felt like play. But she wanted to make sure that being in that environment was not going to harm her child.

It was subtle, but it was important. Those were the kinds of things that I saw happening around me. We were taught to not let others' animosity and bigotry distract us from what we were trying to achieve. We weren't at school to make friends necessarily or to be popular. We were there to learn. That was the idea that was reinforced.

Because I grew up at the end of the Jim Crow era, during the period of transition, everyone I knew was compelled to manage these complex problems. Some people did more, some people did less, but everybody did something. If you study the history of cities like Montgomery, you begin to appreciate how activism was an expectation for people in this community. When the call went out to stay off the buses, they stayed off. Whether you worked as a janitor, or a teacher, whatever your role, you understood that this problem created by segregation and legal apartheid in America was a weight that was not right, was not fair.

That was very much the thinking when I was a very young child. I grew up in a poor, marginalized, racially segregated community. We all talked about how things should change, how things were unfair. People worked really hard, but didn't reap the benefits in the ways that they should have. And so this need for change, this desire to change was communal.

I was fortunate to be raised by people who could tell stories about fore-parents who did extraordinary things. It absolutely motivated me. My grandmother was the daughter of people who were enslaved, and she had a very rich oral history that she shared with us. I was aware of the legacy of lynching because my grandparents talked about what it was like to live in a community where mob violence could threaten and take the life of someone at a moment's notice on something that was just a whim—the harshness of segregation.

Knowing that my great-grandfather had learned to read while en- slaved was enormously impactful for me. He had no reason to expect that he would be free while enslaved in Virginia in the 1850s. Yet he had that belief, that dream, that aspiration, and learning to read had a real impact on the people that he knew and loved. After Emancipa- tion, they would come to his home each week and he would read the newspaper. And my grandmother talked about how inspiring that was for her. Even though educational opportunities were not available, she learned to read and was quite literate. She had ten children, and she made sure all of them were readers.

My mom was the youngest of those ten kids. And even though we grew up poor and had a lot of challenges, she went into debt to buy the *World Book Encyclopedia* for us so we'd have this kind of lens on a greater world outside of our poor community. It reinforced for me that there was something better waiting for us, but we were going to have to fight for it, work for it. I think that shaped my education.

I started in a racially segregated school. Integration came when I was an elementary student. We had to go through that barrier and that came with some challenges. We knew that many people would judge us unfairly if we did not push hard.

As a young person, I wasn't thinking about achievement per se. But I was thinking about how my dad couldn't go to high school in our county in southern Delaware because there were no high schools for black kids when he was a teenager. He was denied that opportunity, so I wanted to take advantage of the opportunity that the generation before had created for me.

I didn't realize I wanted to be a lawyer until much later, but I remember when the lawyers came in and made our community open up the public schools to black kids like me. If not for that, I wouldn't be where I was. That idea that lawyers could have an impact—even when the majority of people didn't want change, they could protect the rights of disfavored people, marginalized people—that was really powerful to me. And that ultimately inspired me to want to be a lawyer and led me to Harvard Law School.

I should say that when I started college, I was just seeing this whole new world of other things to do and had stopped thinking about the law. I was very active in sports and music and loved literature. I was a Philosophy major.

Then, when I was a senior, somebody said to me, "Bryan, you know nobody's gonna pay you to philosophize when you graduate. What are you going to do?" I hadn't really considered what came next, so I started looking into graduate programs. I was a little intimidated because the programs in History or English or Political Science really demanded a high level of knowledge in those disciplines. And I wasn't really preparing for that.

I joke that that's when I decided to go to law school. Because I realized that you don't need to know anything to go to law school. You just have to get in somewhere.

When I got to law school, I was a little taken aback because I'd never met a lawyer in my life. I was there because I wanted to do something about racial injustice, about social inequality, about the problems of the poor and the disenfranchised. But it didn't really seem like anybody was focusing on those issues. They talked about Contracts and Torts and Property and Civil Procedure absent of any awareness of the problems of the poor and people of color. This seemed like it was disconnected from this critical history.

I'll give you a specific example. I remember sitting in an Evidence class where the case was about arresting a young black man suspected of committing a robbery because he had two or three stockings in his bedroom. It was about probable cause. The whole class was completely persuaded that this person must be guilty because he had these stockings.

I remember never really wanting to talk in class, but finally just being so enraged that I raised my hand. I'm not even sure I raised my hand; I may have just shouted out. And I said, "I have stockings in my dresser drawer, and lots of black men put stockings over their heads for a certain kind of hairstyle. And it would be wildly irresponsible for someone to conclude that if they find a stocking in a black male's bedroom that means that they are engaged in robbery. It's that kind of bigotry that leads to wrongful arrests." I remember just kind of giving this mini-lecture, and people were really quiet and staring at me. But it's a reflection of the ways in which the absence of diversity in educational environments can sometimes feed a lot of the problematic thinking that we encounter.

I was pretty disillusioned, so I ended up enlisting in a joint degree program with the School of Government at Harvard. That wasn't any better. I remember a day two months into that program when I woke up and looked in the mirror and thought, *Wow. I'm even more miserable here than I was in the law school.* So I finished my year there and went back to the law school for my second year. I had the opportunity to take a course that required us to spend a month with an organization providing legal services, and that's when things really changed for me. I went to Atlanta to work with what was then called the Southern Prisoners Defense Committee.

That's where I met condemned people on death row for the first time. And it was the proximity of being with the condemned—being with people who were literally dying for legal assistance, being with people who I had been told were beyond hope, beyond redemption, beyond forgiveness to the point where they were going to be executed—that it began to hit me that this was an area where all of the things that had been important to me could come together.

This was in the early 1980s, at the beginning of the era of mass incarceration, when the rates of imprisonment were increasing dramatically. The prison population was about 200,000 in the early 1970s and has risen steadily to 2.3 million today. It just became very clear to me that there was a community of people who were in urgent need of help, who were disproportionately black, who were all poor, and they were on death row.

The idea that we were killing people to show that killing is wrong, just struck me as completely illogical. I came from a faith tradition that reinforced this idea that we are all more than the worst thing we've ever done. I had never doubted that if someone tells a lie, they're not just a liar. If someone takes something, they're not just a thief. I think even if you kill someone, you're not just a killer. That belief made the prospect that these people I met would be executed completely unacceptable.

This experience intensified my desire to be a lawyer. It was actually being on death row and hearing a condemned man—meeting a condemned man, talking to him for three hours and then hearing him sing—that really radicalized my interest in the law. I went back to Harvard and you couldn't get me out of the library. I needed to know everything necessary to equip me to help condemned people avoid execution, to help wrongly convicted people obtain freedom, to help people unfairly sentenced get justice. It was that experience that put me on the path that I've been on, eventually leading to the founding of the Equal Justice Initiative In Montgomery in 1989. Our purpose is simple: to provide legal representation to those who have been denied a fair trial.

I stand on the shoulders of people who did so much more with so much less. The people who came before me would put on their Sunday best to go places and to push for the right to vote and to push against Jim Crow. They'd be on their knees praying, knowing that they were going get battered and bloodied and beaten, and they still went.

It took courage—and that courage inspires and sustains me. I want to encourage law students to create a path in the world that will advance justice. I just think that's important. And that's why I talk a lot about staying proximate to the communities you want to serve, looking for opportunities that will expose you to the kind of work you want to do.

You really do have to be willing to do things that are uncomfortable. If you come out of law school only wanting comfort and convenience, you'll be able to find that to a certain extent. But it may not come with fulfillment. And if what fulfills you and engages you is the pursuit of justice, then I recommend standing with the condemned, the incarcerated, the poor, the hungry, and the homeless:

It will not always be easy, but doing justice is often hard in a world where injustice and inequality have persisted for so long. But you should have faith in your ability to make a difference. I am witness that you can sometimes do a lot with a little—that the ideas in your mind are important, but it's ultimately the conviction in your heart that makes a difference.

FOR MORE INFORMATION:
Eji.org
Bryan Stevenson's book: *Just Mercy*. 2014.

'I Am Undocumented'

ERIKA ANDIOLA, *35, is an immigration rights activist located in metropolitan Phoenix. Much of her work has been driven by her own journey as an undocumented Mexican female immigrant. A graduate of Arizona State University, she was a cofounder of the Arizona Dream Act Coalition and worked as a Latino outreach strategist for Bernie Sanders's 2016 presidential campaign. Most recently she was the chief advocacy officer for RAICES (Refugee and Immigration Center for Education and Legal Services).*

MY MOTHER HAD NEVER done anything wrong. They grabbed her and they handcuffed her and they took her and one of my brothers, too. And I thought: *Maybe this is my fault because I came out on television and said I was undocumented.* I felt so guilty. I was sitting there with my little brother crying, thinking, *What the heck's gonna happen with my mom when she gets deported, Who's gonna help her at the border. What's gonna happen to my brother. Is he gonna be there for a long time?* I didn't know what to do. One of my friends came over, and he said," Erika, you need to stop crying right now. At this moment you are not Erika, the daughter. You're not Erika, the sister. Your mom doesn't need those. You need to be Erika, the activist. You need to get up, and you need to do something about it."

I am undocumented. I am unafraid and I am unashamed. It wasn't always like that. When I first came to this country from Mexico in 1999, I was eleven years old, and you know, it didn't just take me a few steps to get here. It took us three days.

My mom decided to take that journey because she was going through horrible pain caused by my own father. As a strong, amazing woman who cared more about her children, she decided to apply for a visa to come to the United States. Unfortunately, we didn't have the resources to help us prove that we were not going to permanently stay in the U.S. So we got denied a visa many times, and my mom continued to be abused by my own father. We moved, but he followed us. Finally, my mother said, "I need to break this." And she made the toughest decision of her life. We could have been killed trying to get here. We could have been lost in the desert, but she said, "We have to figure out a way to get out of this violence."

We crossed the desert for three days and got to Arizona. I didn't understand how difficult it was going to be to be an undocumented person in the state. I learned English quickly, made friendships, played soccer, joined school clubs. I was starting to feel I was part of this country. It was harder for my mom. To support us she would sell Mexican food door to door or in parking lots.

I worked hard in school and got into Arizona State University, despite my undocumented status. It sounds funny, but I really thought perhaps being a university student, having my ASU ID that I carried everywhere, it kind of felt like a green card that would protect me. But then in 2006, my sophomore year, Arizona passed Proposition 300 that said that if you were undocumented and if you had any scholarships from the state at ASU or other universities, then you couldn't keep them. I was told, "If you don't have a social security number, I'm sorry, but you cannot keep your scholarship."

In 2007, the U.S. Congress began debating the DREAM Act, a bill that would have eliminated that problem and even bigger problems undocumented young people faced—the inability to find work and deportation. It would grant citizenship to undocumented youth who worked very hard, who had graduated from college or gone to the military, etcetera, with all kinds of other requirements and background checks.

About that time, I joined a group of other undocumented students interested in fighting for immigrant rights. Just seeing everything that was being done to my own family was enough to start me figuring out how I could best help them and others who were also suffering injustices. And then, when I couldn't get scholarships and was almost not able to continue school because of my status, that really got me angry.

From the beginning our student group recognized that there was this perception of immigrants and especially undocumented immigrants that was both hurtful to watch personally and hurtful to our cause. On television, people talked about undocumented people in very dehumanizing ways. Now they call us "dreamers," but before then it was just all "illegal aliens" and "criminals." They showed pictures of people trying to cross the border with backpacks on and said they were smuggling drugs. But the truth was those backpacks contained clothes, not contraband.

We determined that we had to change that narrative, had to tell our own stories instead of letting others tell stories that weren't true and hurt our cause. But remember we were undocumented. So in going public, we risked being deported ourselves.

Still, we all said, "It's time for us to come out and give the public the face of the real undocumented people. This is us. This is people who are not stealing anything. This is people who are here to make literally a better life. And we are here to show you who we are. We're gonna tell you our story." Storytelling is so important to any movement.

We said, "We're gonna come out of the shadows. We aren't ashamed." And we formed what we called the Dreamer Movement. We told our story in YouTube videos and on Facebook and Twitter, which were just starting up.

People were so in awe when they saw those videos. Real stories from real people willing to risk deportation. We were building a movement across the country, not just on social media, but with rallies, protests, even civil disobedience. We would literally put our bodies on the line to tell people: "if you really want to deport me, here I am. If you really think I'm a terrible human being coming into this country and seeking a better life for me and my family, then here I am, deport me." And, they didn›t. Gradually, the media started covering us differently—more positively, more accurately.

Unfortunately the DREAM Act failed by five votes in 2010, but we came out of that knowing we had put in place our own system to stop deportation. Somebody would call us and say, "I'm in trouble. Immigration came and they took me. I need to figure out how to stay here." Or their families would call us. And we were able to stop their deportations by organizing the community, by making thousands of calls to Immigration, by making thousands of calls to our Congress members.

Finally on June 15, 2012, because of the movement that we created, President Obama issued an executive order for Deferred Action for Childhood Arrivals, DACA. It's not a path to citizenship. It's a work permit. It's something that allows you to stay here. I was able to apply, and I was able to get a work permit. And for the first time ever, I had a social security number.

By changing the narrative, especially for young immigrants, we were able to see policy changes. When you get wins like that for your community, that's when you know that storytelling is making an impact .

Not long after I got my social security number, I got a call from then-Arizona Congresswoman Kyrsten Sinema, whom I had previously worked with to fight another law. She said she wanted to hire a Dreamer. "You wanna work in Congress?"

I said, "Why not? Let's pass immigration reform."

I called home and said, "Mommy, we should cook something or go out to dinner, because I just got a job in Congress."

When I came home, my mom said, "I'm gonna take a shower so we can go celebrate." And while she was taking that shower, I got a knock on the door. And that's when they took my mom and brother.

I did become *Erika, the activist.* In a matter of twelve hours, we organized thousands of people throughout the country. I put up a YouTube video which got about sixty thousand views (https://www .youtube.com/watch?v=FVZKfoXsMxk).

People made thousands of calls because they saw it. And at 9 a.m. the next morning, I got a call from the Mexican consulate. They said, "We have somebody here. Her name is Maria." And my mom said she had just been returned. She's coming home.

Getting off the couch, mobilizing, mattered. I think being an activist is being able to feel and see the injustices that are around you and your own life experience. You love the people you care about, people in your community, and then take the step of doing something about those injustices. Activism is being able to use your own voice, to use any power that you may have, to marshal the people in your community who want to join you and address the injustices in front of you. That's how I started. I started seeing what was going on in my own community and decided to do something about it.

If you feel like it's the right thing to do, you would be surprised at how many people will feel inspired and motivated to also speak up with you. So my advice would be: if you're thinking about taking the first step, do it! But don't necessarily go out and do something crazy by yourself without building the support that you need. You don't have to be the only voice. I assure you, there's going to be a lot more people on your campus or your school that are thinking about some of the same issues as you.

That's where organizing comes into play. You look around and find those other people and get together and figure out, *How can we start raising our voices together*? That's how we started; a few of us began speaking out and eventually grew into a movement of undocumented youth that actually got the President of the United States to do something.

Whatever your cause, you have to try to address it in the best way that works for you. In my case, working in Congress wasn't me. I felt I was dealing more with "issues" than the people who were really being impacted. When I had the chance to join Bernie Sanders's 2016 presidential campaign as a Latino outreach strategist, I said, "I gotta jump on that train. I gotta figure out we can do for immigration." I think that was very useful, but again, it was not necessarily working with the people that are directly impacted.

In the end, I found that working at an immigrants' rights organization like RAICES was best for me. I was back in the space working with folks whose stories I know. I know who they are and the real suffering they are going through. I needed to feel more rooted in the struggle than being on Capitol Hill or in a political campaign.

I'm an immigrant and could still be deported. My family could still be deported. That really grounds me. RAICES works with new arrivals, asylum seekers, refugees, and with the immigrant community that has been here for many years, like my family. There's an array of issues that are within the immigration space that are not just policy. In Washington, it seems like every issue is just like a card on the table that you're gonna try to figure out how to play it. But we aren't cards. We are human beings.

FOR MORE INFORMATION:
raicestexas.org

'Breaking Down Stereotypes'

AMIRAH AHMED, 18, *cofounded Fredericksburg Muslim Youth (FMY) in 2020 while a high school student in Fredericksburg, Virginia. She is a member of the Class of 2025 at the University of Mary Washington in Fredericksburg.*

I REMEMBER STAYING UP the night of the 2016 presidential election. It was a pivotal moment. I was twelve, in eighth grade. I didn't understand everything that was going on, but I did know the result held so much emotion and consequence, particularly for Muslim Americans like our family. I remember the results coming in and just sitting in the bathroom, sobbing.

I was born and raised in a diverse community in New Orleans. My mom is a white, agnostic woman, and my dad is a Muslim Arab man, born in the United States. His parents, my grandparents, had emigrated here from Egypt. I grew up speaking Arabic, and in a community that practiced my culture, but I didn't consciously think, *I'm Arab* or *I'm Muslim*. It was just a part of who I was.

We moved to Virginia right before middle school started, and that's when I began to navigate my identity. I didn't wear the hijab, so I was not visibly Muslim, and the only thing I would say that gave me away as *other*, would be my name. A lot of the time, especially without hijab, I'm a white-passing woman. But the school was primarily white—as opposed to the school I'd gone to in New Orleans. So that's where I found my *otherness*, and realized that I wasn't the same as everybody else.

Whenever we talked about 9/11 or terrorism in school, people recognized that I was super *other*. But I never got bullied or anything. It was just the micro-aggressions that I think a lot of us are normalized to when we're young. We don't see anything wrong with it, because that's how everybody talks to us. And I guess now we're kind of unlearning that stuff collectively as a culture or community.

Eighth grade was when I started to take pride in my identity and ownership in who I was. The election changed everything for everyone. Trump had run on an anti-Muslim platform, and as soon as he took office, he instituted the Muslim ban. We were talking about it in classes, and identity was a topic of discussion for everyone, not just for Muslims and Arabs.

I started writing poetry that year and sharing it. I just kind of verbally started putting myself out there. Once I started reflecting, that's when questions and past and present experiences with Islamophobia started to come in.

We moved within Virginia to Fredericksburg right before freshman year of high school, and that's when I started wearing the hijab. I didn't know anybody and it was like, *I'm coming in with a fresh start. I'll wear the hijab.* I wanted to create something for myself, and see what I could do to create change in this new Trump era. Honestly, it wasn't a decision based so much on my personal faith. I was seeing what was going on around me, and I saw all these other women that were visibly Muslim women that were sticking up for our rights and amplifying our voices. I thought that was so brave, and I wanted to be a part of that.

My high school had a majority of minority students. It was a great environment to navigate my activism. I define activism as any effort towards change for a larger issue. A lot of time when people think of activism, they think protests, large-scale resistance. Obviously, that's a part of activism, and that's wonderful, but that's not always realistic. Not everybody can take to the streets. It's not always accessible to young people. Especially if you're coming from a culture like mine, where your parents would never let you go to a protest and do something like that.

I started out small and very grassroots. I was passionate about climate change, so I started an environmentalism club. In eighth grade I fell in love with slam poetry. It's such a powerful way of expressing your thoughts and feelings, especially whenever we're talking about political events or situations that concern our identity. So I started my own poetry club at school, and we hosted different slams and events. I also started performing my poetry. My spoken word is very culturally and politically driven. And it's definitely been a vehicle for my activism. Here's a passage from my poem "Hypocrisy," which I first performed in 2018.

> Discriminate against Muslim
> women and our veils,
> the same veil that. . .Virgin Mary
> wore? and it's okay when nuns
> wear it, right?
> But hey,
> I'm not here to
> hate. I can't
> resent you or
> hate you
> because the same religion you call
> distasteful has taught me that
> it is wrong to do so.

There was so much happening everywhere after the election. At our school I participated in walkouts and lay-ins. I wasn't necessarily an organizer, but I would join in to protest things like school shootings and gun violence.

My best friend was and still is Amatul Musawir. She was the only other hijabi woman in our class, and we instantly clicked. Our sophomore year, we hosted a Muslim Women's Day event. Muslim Women's Day was created in 2017 by Amani Al-Khatahtbeh. She's the founder of muslimgirl.com and an icon for Muslim girls in the U.S. even though she just turned thirty this year. We did a school event in the library with a Q and A and food. It was really awesome. It brought a lot of awareness, because there weren't a lot of visibly Muslim women or just Muslims at our school.

At the same time, we were talking about trying to start something for the Muslim youth in our community. There wasn't anything at the mosque or the school. So we said, "Okay, we're just going to have to create it ourselves."

In April 2020 we founded Fredericksburg Muslim Youth, which is my biggest catalyst for my activism now. It was just us, a two person team. The hardest part was just trying to find people. Finding the Muslims in Fredericksburg is a very hard task, and we didn't really have the support of the mosque at that point.

We worked with what we had. We used social media to set up some virtual speaker sessions. The numbers were really low, as you can imagine. I think the most we had at one event was fifteen people. And a lot of the time they weren't even youth. They were just community members that we had reached out to. Organizing work is hard. We created our website and our Instagram and reached out to as many Muslims as possible.

There are a lot of immigrant families in our area, and a lot of them are low income and can't afford tutoring. We wanted to do something, not only for the people in our Muslim community, but just the larger Fredericksburg community. So in December 2020, we started a free K-12 tutoring service that's powered by high school volunteers, almost all of whom are not Muslim.

That program is one of the biggest things that I've done, impact-wise. It's something that we still do every single week. That success helped us reach out and find a lot more Muslim youth for membership with FMY. And we also began a partnership with the Islamic

Center of Fredericksburg. We are still a sovereign organization, but we also serve as their youth branch. That helps us expand our reach a little bit more.

The summer of 2020, when George Floyd was murdered, was a huge moment for a lot of activists in my generation. I credit the Black Lives Matter movement for spurring a lot of action in many different communities. I became involved with a lot of organizations working for social justice. It was a pivotal time for me because I was educating myself about a lot of issues.

That summer I also worked on the political campaign of the woman who had become big part of my activism journey: Amani Al-Khatahtbeh. When she ran for Congress in New Jersey in 2020, I joined her effort as the events team leader. Unfortunately, she lost, but she's become like a mentor for me.

With all of these activities, I think I was coming into my power and understanding of what I can do, where my place is as a Muslim Arab woman in the U.S. and in the activism world.

During our senior year, in March 2021, Amatul and I decided to do Muslim Women's day again—this time for more than just students and teachers at our high school. We were like, "Now we have this platform, we have FMY. We can use this organization as a catalyst to do something bigger, that will have a bigger reach."

We reached out to potential panelists. At first we thought we'd look locally, thinking, *We don't really have that much influence, yet. We're barely a year old as an organization.* But then we decided to be super-ambitious. We reached out to people that we never thought would ever actually respond, but lo and behold, they did! And we got seven amazing panelists, including Linda Sarsour. You probably know she's a leading Arab activist who co-chaired the 2017 Women's March.

I remember the day that she responded to our email. We sat there and just screamed for an hour. Same thing with some of the others who agreed to participate. We were like, "Oh my goodness, there's no way," because these are the people that raised us. These are the Muslim women that we saw in the media. The title was "Muslim Women Breaking Down Stereotypes," and it was one of the biggest, most impactful things that I've done in my activism journey.

I started college at American University in D.C., which is very politically active. I got involved with the Sunrise Movement, which is an environmental activism group, as well as the Muslim Student Association. It's not an inherently political group, but they do a lot of activism and organizing work for the Muslim community and Muslim Americans in general, as well as Palestine. After my freshman year I transferred to the University of Mary Washington so I could be closer to Fredericksburg and focus on FMY activities.

My advice to young people who want to become activists is: first, it's okay to start small. Don't align yourself with a national organization just because it has a big name that might look good on your resume. Grassroots activism is great. Don't overlook the change that you can make on a local level. Look to your right and your left and see your peers and your family and community members; they're the ones that also need help. Campaigning to get that resource from the school board or from your local government, that's impactful. Just because you're not on the streets of Washington, doesn't mean that it's not making a difference.

Whatever you're working towards, you have to build it on resilience. Because for that first year especially, sometimes you're going to have events where you show up, and it's going to be you and the other person that organized the event. Nobody's going to show up, and you have to be okay with failure. You're going to fail a lot, a lot. But that is the essence of organizing and of activism. Change does not come from just snapping our fingers and putting out a social media post, and then it's there. It takes the work.

Keeping the bigger picture in mind at all times is important—being able to reflect and look back, even after your failures, look around and say, "Okay, is my cause where I want it to be? Is the problem fixed? No? Okay, I have to keep going."

FOR MORE INFORMATION:
https://fxburgmy.wixsite.com/fxburgmuslimyouth
https://www.instagram.com/fxburgmuslimyouth/
https://linktr.ee/amiraharielle

'To Access the Hub'

ZEV SHAPIRO, *20, grew up in Cambridge, Massachusetts. Currently a junior at Harvard, he is the founder and executive director of TurnUp, a nonprofit organization and mobile app focused on increasing youth voter turnout and activism.*

WHEN I WAS IN fourth grade, a lot of my friends were complaining about the food at our elementary school. I thought, *This isn't fair*. Most people were not able to bring lunch from home like I was. I thought we should have a healthy option. So I created a petition and solicited support from other individuals. My argument even included some helpful tips, such as: "The designers would have to consider how high off the ground it should be so the little kids could reach. Also they would have to consider how hot the soup should be so people won't burn themselves."

The petition was successful, unanimously approved by school officials, and we got a salad bar. Because it was a success, I started to think I'd actually be able to make a difference, that I'd be able to impact change again.

When I was about nine, I started listening to the portable radio in my bedroom. I listened to NPR quite a bit. My mom Nancy Shapiro would also put NPR on when we were in the car. So I started paying attention to the news. One day I heard Elizabeth Warren. I thought what she was saying was interesting and that maybe I could get involved in her campaign for the Senate. This was 2012.

I wrote a pretty long letter to the campaign telling them why I thought I would be qualified to volunteer. I figured maybe they wouldn't think

that I would be because I was only nine. So I explained some of the
things I'd done—like getting the salad bar at our school.

> Chaperoned by his grandmother, Shapiro canvassed door to door.
> Bitten by the campaign bug, he also volunteered in the successful
> campaigns of Ed Markey for Senate and Maura Healey for Massa-
> chusetts Attorney General. At the age of eleven, he actually managed
> the campaign of Joyce Gerber, a candidate for the Cambridge School
> Committee. Gerber sang his praises, noting that, "He understands
> the numbers. . .and knows how to use the data." In 2014, Senator
> Warren invited Shapiro to be her guest at President Obama's State of
> the Union Address.

I worked on the campaigns of different candidates I liked until 2016,
but then sort of adjusted a bit. I became much more involved and really
passionate about youth civic engagement. Issues are important to me,
but the number one thing I care about is strengthening our democracy.
I believe in it; it works really well when our voices are heard. But I really feel that our system is at risk.

So after working on those campaigns, I felt that working with young
people was an area where I had the ability to make the largest impact.
At that point I had been out in the world working with a lot of adults
and felt I could translate that into determining how young people
could be supported to participate in civic opportunities—whether it
was in campaigns or just learning about how our government works.

I saw there was this problem in schools. Students weren't learning
civics. One of my friends who was very knowledgeable didn't even
know that there were three branches of government; I had to teach
her. And this is in Cambridge! I was amazed. Adults were not necessarily aware of this situation, because when they were in school,
many of them did learn civics.

At this time there was an effort going on to push civics education in Massachusetts. I asked myself how I could participate. One of the biggest problems we have in this country is polarization. So I created a partnership between Massachusetts High School Democrats and Massachusetts High School Republicans with the idea that we could work together to push for the bill requiring civics education in the schools.

We met with many of the important Massachusetts legislators. We got a lot of publicity. And we made a difference. The bill passed.

I started thinking about other avenues for strengthening our democracy through increasing youth involvement. My philosophy of life is that everybody should at least have the opportunity to participate civically, to have the opportunity to learn about how our government works so that then they can vote. Looking around, I saw that a lot of the upcoming 2018 congressional political campaigns were not catering to young people. I talked with others in the High School Democrats of America and asked, "Can we develop resources? Could high school students have the same opportunities I had?" If you can work as an intern on a campaign, you'll learn so much.

We ended up promoting internship opportunities to Democratic organizations and politicians. We created a sort of guidebook that showed students how to connect with local leaders. We said, "This is what a successful program looks like. This is why it's important. These are sample internship applications. We were able to say, "If you're a young person, more campaigns will have a place for you as an intern." We provided resources for about forty key races.

Around this time the Parkland shootings happened in Florida. This was tragic. But something very inspiring came out of the tragedy. Millions of people—especially young people—wanted to get involved for the first time. A lot of them weren't sure how to do that. I knew other people like myself who had tried in the past to involve young people. After Parkland, we were asking, "How do we do that now?"

There were lots of events going on, but those of us in Cambridge didn't even know what was going on in Boston. We also didn't know what students were in involved. The only thing that everybody knew about was the National March in Washington.

So here was another challenge: A lot of people wanted to get involved, but they didn't know how. That was really disappointing to me because I feel strongly if a young person wants to do something, they really should be able to. It made me really sad that there were people in Cambridge who wanted to make change, but they couldn't even figure out what was going on in Boston. Even if it wasn't that they were interested in gun control—maybe it was climate change or other issues—they couldn't easily figure out what was going on where.

The reason for this is because we young people are not using Facebook, which is a common organizing tool of other generations. We use Snapchat, Instagram, TikTok, but everything disappears on those platforms. They're not purpose-built for organizing. So I thought: *What if there were a way for people to access the hub for events, community connection, educational resources about activism and issues?*

That was the idea, so we studied other platforms to see whether we could use something that already existed. We found there might be one app for registering to vote, another app for education about activism, another app for group chat. It was all spread out. There was no single location to learn about how to get involved and where to get involved when you want to.

I wasn't an entrepreneur or an app developer; my interests are politics and civic engagement. And baroque music! After thinking about it for a while, I put together an advisory board of people who are well known and very knowledgeable in different and related fields such as digital security and fundraising, people who are long-time activists, people in app development. This was possible because of the credentials I had from my political work and the connections I had made, and through a lot of emailing and networking. Almost everyone we contacted said, "Yes." Beginning in 2019, after we had a board with great credentials and credibility, we started raising money for this because we needed to hire a developer.

I love technology, too. But for me, this was simply the means to achieving a stronger democracy where more people would have the opportunity to get involved. I didn't know a lot of about startups at that point. I had to learn a lot.

We decided to be a tech nonprofit and register as a 501c3 charity. App development alone took about a year—basically from the summer of 2019 to the summer of 2020. It was very complicated.

During that time, the pandemic started. That changed everything. We've focused on many different areas that I never expected. People should visit the TurnUp website to see all that we do. In short, we have internship programs where we train people for advocacy and engagement projects. We offer tools for organization and education. And we do voter registration and turnout. In the 2021 Georgia runoff election, we were by far the largest youth-led, youth-voter turnout operation.

Our outreach includes speaking engagements. My message is: you can make a difference. Learn what is going on, think about what you could do about it, talk about the issues. Also, be prepared. There are going to be a lot of challenges and obstacles. it's really about perseverance. Don't just show up, but persevere,

Recognize that young people—specifically those closely connected to an issue—have a very important and relevant perspective that others might not have. So if you see an issue, appreciate your power and show up.

There was nothing out there like us when we started. And now there's so much more to TurnUp. We have a lot of priorities coming up. We have created a fund to invest in ideas from young people who are focused on increasing civic engagement and voter turnout and activism. We want to support those ideas. We actually have a tool now that allows a person to figure out where their vote will be more valuable—whether it's in their home state or where they go to school. That was developed by young people. We're really trying to think about all the possible ways we can increase youth engagement to strengthen democracy. We're trying to hire people to organize voter registration in high schools, where efforts have lacked in comparison to college,

For myself, this is my career. It's interesting. I mean, I've been doing this political stuff now for ten years. I'm going to continue with it in terms of youth civic engagement. I'm open to changing that focus if I'm shown there's another way that I can make a bigger impact on our democracy, but I don't think that's going to be the case. So I expect to focus on this for the foreseeable future.

FOR MORE INFORMATION:

www.turnup.us

Nancy Shapiro's book: *An ABC of Democracy*, 2022

'Poetry Could Do Something'

ASHLEY M. JONES, *32, is poet laureate of the state of Alabama (2022–2026). She received an MFA in Poetry from Florida International University. She currently lives in Birmingham, Alabama, where she is founding director of the Magic City Poetry Festival and a faculty member in the Creative Writing Department of the Alabama School of Fine Arts.*

YOU LOOK AT THE history and wonder: *What would I have done? Would I have been one of those children marching in Birmingham in 1963? Would I have marched over the Edmund Pettus bridge from Selma to Montgomery in 1965?* I never really knew what that would look like for me. I am very anxious around police or any sort of dangerous situation.

And then in 2020, George Floyd was murdered and everyone mobilized. Luckily I had just taught *March* by John Lewis. And I thought, *Okay, this movement had so many pieces to it.* We, of course, see the images of those who were on the ground doing sit-ins and protesting, but there was a whole network of people making sure the structure was there. People working in offices, writing letters, getting food together. So I figured out that where my strengths lie in the movement is with my writing and with my ability to organize people around a cause.

I was totally aware of my history from an early age. My dad was part of a school integration growing up in Bessemer, Alabama. My parents made sure that we interacted with blackness all the time. My dad painted a Santa Claus brown because we couldn't find one in the stores. We were allowed to imagine our God looking like us.

I've been writing poetry since I was seven. The poem that turned me toward that is called, "Harriet Tubman." It's by Eloise Greenfield and is from a book called, *Honey, I Love.* I love that book. It's sort of radical because it celebrates black existence, black joy. So my beginning was reciting this piece about Harriet Tubman, who freed so many slaves. And from there I started writing poems about everything, including racism.

I went to a fine arts high school in Birmingham where there weren't that many black students in my department. I got away from writing about social issues for a while. I was just trying to sound like the other kids basically. But then I read Rita Dove's *Selected Poems.*

Reading that book showed me that I could write about my own people. Then in college I found my poetry patron saint, Lucille Clifton. Her work pushed me even further back into my authentic self. So it was finding people who were like me and understanding that they gave us permission to write about ourselves. As people of color, we have to do that on our own because we don't necessarily get that in the traditional education system.

I knew that poetry had some changing power for me personally, but it was really at the end of graduate school in South Florida when I cemented the idea that it could effect social change. I was working with young people in a spoken word project and saw this was making a change in their lives. I could see in them a sort of a confidence being born as they wrote, instead of just reading other people's words. Having the opportunity to speak and be listened to. I started to understand that it's really important for any child, but especially for children of color, to feel like their opinions matter and that people will listen to them.

When I came back home to Birmingham, I started working with a wonderful worldwide program called One Hundred Thousand Poets for Change. On the last Saturday of September, we have an event where people share poetry that has a social justice theme. In Birmingham we added an element where we do fundraising for organizations.

One year we worked with a group involved in immigrant justice. They were trying to get people out of the Etowah County Detention

Center, which is one of the worst in the nation. We had two events where we were reading poems about justice, and we had one of the organization's representatives read some letters from people who were detained.

After this event, we were able to raise over one thousand dollars—enough to help free somebody from the detention center. Incredible! For me it was, *Okay, I was right.* I knew that poetry could do something. And here, now, I had something tangible. Our words changed people's hearts to give money and to change someone's life to let them go free.

Since then, we've kept raising money. I wish we didn't live in a society where money meant anything, but because it does, we're going to use our art form to help free people or to help in other ways.

Also since returning I started a nonprofit, the Magic City Poetry Festival. In 2020, we did a fundraiser where if you show us the receipt for a donation you made to a liberation or human service organization, we'll write a poem for you. So this is where I've really found myself in being an activist.

I write poems on many subjects, including myself and historical pieces. With some poems I've had to understand the moment I'm writing about. In my first book, *Magic City Gospel*, there are a lot of poems about the civil rights movement. I immersed myself, watching videos of Bull Connor at the Children's March in Birmingham or of the segregationist Alabama Governor George Wallace. It's scary when you realize, *Oh, wait, these are humans doing things to other humans.*

In a couple of poems about Wallace, I had to get deep into his life to understand his motivations. Looking at the facts, I could sort of see in between them. That's where the poetry comes in—to look at, for example, an image of Wallace standing in the schoolhouse door on June 11, 1963, trying to block desegregating the University of Alabama. Looking at his body and seeing something as small as his suit jacket being buttoned incorrectly, that's where the poetry allowed me to open up that moment and say, "Maybe he was nervous. Maybe he was rushed."

Facts aren't a trap. They allow the creativity to bloom. At the same time, I don't really feel like I have the liberty to make things up. I don't want people to dismiss or be able to say, "Well, you're just exaggerating." People love to tell a black person that it's not that bad, you know?

I titled my poem about that day, "Rammer Jammer":

> Between the thighs
> of the doorway,
> you are powerful.
> The confetti of camera clicks
> and your smart business suit
> and the swamp of teenaged protesters
> swaddle you with sweat.
> June in Alabama is rife with heat.
> Important men from Washington have come
> to clear you out.
> Tension,
> thick and bitter
> as a watermelon rind.
> From the doorway,
> you see Vivian and James
> waiting in the government car.
> They wish to register here.
> From the doorway,
> you see walls and waves of
> ballot-faced whites. They are checkmarks
> in the next election.
> It is only after
> your speech is delivered that you realize how thirsty you are—
> your cottonmouth
> is unbecoming
> for a state leader.

How nice it would be
to sit on your porch
with Lurleen and a glass of sweet tea.
How nice it would be
to get out of this heat
and out of Tuscaloosa
and back to marbled Montgomery
and its halls that echo—
obedient, loud, and white.

I teach now at the fine arts school I attended. The students are already there to write, so I don't have to fight with them to do that. As for getting them excited to write about social justice, I try to approach the classroom in a way that they feel free to do that. They're not forced per se. We might be writing sonnets, we might be doing meter, whatever. I'm teaching the concept like anyone else might teach it. But it's the example poems that I give that open that door. So instead of reading Shakespeare, we might read a sonnet by Patricia Smith about Emmett Till that allows me to give them the historical context.

There are many more students of color than there were when I was there some fifteen years ago. That's one reason why I wanted to come back—just to be visible and offer another perspective for all the students—because I do think it benefits the white students as well to be able to interact with a teacher of color and to think about some of these issues that they may not have thought about before.

Expressing yourself is so important. It doesn't have to be poetry. Every art form is a way to find your voice. I truly believe that we all are given some avenue to take. Many times I wish I had been given dancing or singing ability, but I was given writing. So that's what I do. The advice I give is to really listen to yourself and hear what it is that you need to do. For me, I hear very clearly when I recite a poem, *this is the thing I need to do.* If you feel in your body, *I must make movement in order to express myself*, then you should listen to it, be authentically who you are.

Storytelling is so vital. At least in America. All of us have been suffering from silence for a really long time. That's why art is so important for me and many of my peers. Because we had art, we could tell our story. So we were able to develop into adults in a different way than some other people. I can make no claims about some of these people who commit horrible crimes against others, but I do wonder: *Did they have a chance to really express themselves in any other way? Is that a way to cut off some of these behaviors or at least to start the empathy making process?*

People of all ages come to workshops or readings, and they say, "I'm glad that you're telling our story," or, "I feel like I can now tell my story." And it always comes back to us just being able to express our humanity.

I've dedicated my career, so far, to honoring my ancestors and what they went through in America—to educating people about what happens to black people in America, and to being my full authentic self on and off the page to make room for others to do the same. I'm hopeful that I can keep that going as poet laureate, and that I can inspire those who see themselves left out, who are marginalized and oppressed, who are constantly fighting for our humanity to be recognized, to continue showing up and speaking out.

Of course, black people have been trying to express that forever, that we are human beings. This system of white supremacy that we are in hurts all of us. None of us are able to fully express ourselves if we are all trying to operate under this ridiculous system or operate under a need for power and money in all of this, when really none of that has anything to do with our souls, our hearts, who we are.

That's what I see in the classroom every day. The students are excited. It's great to be able to say, " I am here. Here is what I feel. Here is who I am." I love being a black woman! I love black women!

We should be celebrated. That in no way detracts from anyone else's worthiness of celebration.

If we could all do that in America, that's a great first step to reparations—because we're self-aware. We can then be more aware of our history and not feel like people are judging us or saying that we are bad because the history exists. If we're able to have those hard conversations, knowing that we both acknowledge our shared humanity, everything I think could fall into place.

FOR MORE INFORMATION:
www.ashleymjonespoetry.com
Her books: *Magic City Gospel*, 2017; *dark//thing*, 2019;
Reparations Now!, 2021

'It's Not Just About Voting'

TRAM NGUYEN, 41, is an award-winning activist and community leader who helped found New Virginia Majority (NVM) in 2007. She currently serves as NVM's co-executive director, where she leads multi-racial, multi-issue campaigns using large-scale civic engagement, community organizing, advocacy, leadership development, and strategic communications.

I REMEMBER WHEN MY family took our very first vacation. I was five years old, and we went to Myrtle Beach, South Carolina, with my cousins. My parents made a lot of sacrifices for us to go. When my sisters, cousins, and I saw a swimming pool for the first time, we jumped in. One of the people in the pool sounded the alarm by referring to us with a racial slur, and everybody else jumped out.

As immigrants, for years growing up, it was like, *You have to just focus on you. Don't rock the boat. Don't make any waves.* And I think as I grew older and started witnessing so many inequities around me and the life experience that I had growing up in Virginia and going to college in New York City—all of that just made me realize that people like me shouldn't keep our heads down. We don't need to. In fact, when we use our voices and we become active right in our communities and tap into that activism, we could really make a difference and change the world. I saw the possibilities.

My family immigrated here in 1981 when I was six months old. We were part of the second wave of boat people, refugees from the Vietnam War. We came to Virginia, which back then was not nearly as diverse as it is today. I remember very vividly being in first grade and my classmates debating in front of me whether I was black or whether I was white, because nobody in the suburbs of Richmond looked like me. I remember asking a lot of my teachers and the adults around me, "What does this all mean?" And the response that I kept getting was, as I've said: "Don't worry about it. Keep your head down. Get good grades and, and you'll be fine."

I was on federal work-study and got a lot of financial aid to be able to go to Barnard College in New York City. My work-study was with the America Reads program. I was tutoring Dominican kids in South Harlem and realized their experiences and challenges growing up as immigrants were similar to mine. Not exactly the same, but we were all trying to figure things out and find ourselves. I built such strong and great relationships with them that I started thinking about the public education system and all of the systemic inequities that exist.

I was a junior when 9/11 happened. That experience was life-changing. From a personal level, many of my friends and I lost people we knew in the South Tower. For weeks, not a day went by that there wasn't some sort of memorial service on campus. You'd see Army tanks going up and down Broadway carrying supplies to Ground Zero. I also witnessed rising tensions and the scapegoating of the Muslim community. That was so wrong in my mind.

All of these experiences really politicized me and made me realize that you can't sit on the sidelines. If you feel that something's not right, if you see something, if you experience something, you've gotta figure out a way to get involved and to push back.

On campus I became active in student leadership and ended up being Vice President for Student Activities of our student government association. I was the one who got to determine which student clubs got recognition, so I worked closely with student groups that supported lifting up the voices of minority populations and figuring out ways to get resources to them.

How did I end up here at New Virginia Majority? I sometimes joke that it's by accident that I fell into this career, but I honestly think that my life sort of made this my destiny. I was an Economics major, and all of my peers at the time were getting these signing bonuses from Goldman Sachs and JP Morgan to go into investment banking. And here I was thinking, *I should do that too, because I've got all this student debt and I need the money.* But I just couldn't.

So my first job out of college was in public health. I worked with a lot of the rescue recovery workers at Mount Sinai Hospital in New York with the World Trade Center Health Program. Under my boss's incredible leadership, I was part of a team that worked with Congresswoman Carolyn Maloney and then Senator Hillary Clinton to try to advocate and push for federal dollars to support these workers who were dealing with severe illnesses. That gave me a taste for what it was like to take an issue and then advocate for some solutions.

After that I ended up moving back to Virginia and started working with an organization that focused more on the Vietnamese community. Going back to that notion that we should just keep our heads down, forget our culture, and assimilate and be quote unquote American, I was now in my twenties, realizing *I'm Vietnamese. I'm Vietnamese-American. I should be proud of my Vietnamese heritage, and I should be more involved in that community.* So I joined an organization called Boat People SOS (BPSOS), a national nonprofit that works directly with Vietnamese communities.

I was hired as director of their AmeriCorps program, but two weeks into my job Hurricane Katrina happened. We got a call from our Houston office, and they said, "We need a lot of help." Thousands of displaced Vietnamese people from New Orleans were going to Houston, which has the third largest Vietnamese population in the country. They were all just lining up at the Hong Kong strip mall, and no one—not the Red Cross or FEMA—was prepared for them.

I guess since I had a 9/11 background they thought I was the person to fly down from Virginia and report what was happening—even though I was only twenty-four. That ended up turning into two-and-a half-years of directing this multimillion-dollar program that worked with the tens of thousands of Vietnamese that ended up in Houston; Biloxi, Mississippi; and Bayou La Batre, Alabama; and needed all sorts of services. At the age of twenty-five, I testified before Congress and worked with fellow advocates to successfully amend the federal Stafford Act to include language and cultural competency in emergency preparedness and response.

I burned out from working in disaster situations. So in 2007, shaped by my experiences of racial discrimination growing up as an immigrant in the south, I helped launch New Virginia Majority to give voice to the most underrepresented among us. This was right after comprehensive immigration reform—which we had all thought had a good chance of passing Congress—failed. Millions of people across the country had marched in support, so when we lost our analysis was that it wasn't enough to just take to the streets and mobilize.

We realized that if we want to really effect change, it's going to take us using all of our tools in our toolbox. Besides protesting, that also means engaging in the electoral arena. Oftentimes it had been easy for politicians to brush off demands coming from the immigrant community because we didn't vote. There was no way to hold our elected officials accountable. So we started this organization to tap into what we thought was an emerging and powerful political force in Virginia.

The demographics have changed so much since I was in the first grade in the 1980s. But demographics isn't destiny. So how do we start to really organize these new American communities across the state? Especially because in many of these communities getting involved in your government is not common for political refugees.

We set out to educate and mobilize new Americans, black and brown people, and young people, not only in the streets, but at the electoral ballot box in a completely nonpartisan way and help people to understand that they do have a voice in ensuring government works for all of us. So over the last fourteen years, we have knocked on over three million doors talking to Virginians about issues like racial equity, democracy, criminal justice reform. We've registered nearly three hundred thousand new voters of color.

People hear our name and they think we're talking about a political majority. But, no. We're talking about a majority of Virginians that better reflects our diversity. It's more about the will of the people, because we can't continue to ignore the role that lack of representation plays in perpetuating a cycle of neglect for women and communities of color.

But it's not just about voting. Elections are never our finish line. If you treat elections as your finish line, then what's the purpose? The work towards building a Virginia that works for all of us has never been about any elected official. The work is within our communities and for our communities—to advance an agenda that supports progress and opportunity, and that promotes a strong and healthy democracy. No matter who gets elected, these elected officials aren't our heroes; we're our own heroes. No matter who gets elected, we continue to mobilize and organize our folks to fight for affordable housing, immigrant rights, reforming our criminal legal system.

Over the last couple of years, we have made such transformative change in our state. Because of the efforts of our organization and a lot of our partner organizations, we became the first state in the South to end the death penalty. We were the first in the South to legalize marijuana. We have made tremendous reforms around expanding voting rights and in immigrant rights—such as allowing undocumented residents to pay in-state tuition for college and being able to get driver-privilege cards that allow them to drive. We passed a law that says racism is a public health issue, and my personal labor of love: we became the first state in the South to pass a state voting rights act at a time when our democracy is under attack across the nation.

Forty years ago, my mom and dad left everyone and everything behind in Vietnam in search of the dream of America, and the promise of freedom, equality and justice that she holds. Forty years ago, my parents weren't even sure they would make it here safely, let alone imagine that the daughter they gave birth to in a refugee camp would grow up to be one of the fiercest defenders of their dream of equality and justice in America.

That dream is only possible if we use our power. I think it's really important to use your voice as often as you can. Even if you think it's small, you never know how that will affect those around you. You might have inspired somebody else to pick up the mantle. The fight for social justice and racial equity takes all of us; we all have our roles to play.

I used to feel guilty for not showing up to every march. And then I realized: *I don't have to show up to every march because there are so many of us that are fighting alongside each other for the same thing.*

Don't feel like you have to carry the weight of the world on your own shoulders; there are so many of us with you. Whether it's in your own little community, your own neighborhood, your own street, your own classroom, or if it's on a larger scale, we all have a role to play. If we're all in it together, we can build upon each other.

FOR MORE INFORMATION:
www.newvirginiamajority.org

'Standing in My Own Driveway'

DOUG GLANVILLE, 52, *has worn many hats. As the first African American graduate of an Ivy League college (University of Pennsylvania) to play major league baseball, he patrolled the outfield for nine seasons before retiring in 2004. Since then he has written for the* New York Times, The Atlantic, *and other major publications and has written a book about baseball (*The Game from Where I Stand*); taught social justice-related courses at Penn, Yale, and the University of Connecticut; and worked in-studio and in the broadcast booth for ESPN.*

WHEN I WAS FIVE or six, I was at summer camp and we were supposed to sit in a circle and hold hands. The kid next to me refused. He said something like, "I don't hold hands with darkies."

The thing that was so powerful about that moment was that I didn't actually internalize it. I didn't think, *Oh, I'm bad.* It was more like, *What's wrong with him?* I remember the counselors whisked me away. They were horrified. I told them, "I'm okay. It's his problem."

My dad was from Trinidad and came to the United States in the mid-1950s as a thirty-one-year-old freshman at Howard University, after he had been long-established as a teacher. He came with a certain hope beyond the words and tenets of America—believing in this opportunity to live them and holding America to them. He eventually got his medical degree and established a psychiatric practice.

My mom was raised in the Jim Crow South. She was a born teacher, embracing her parents' emphasis on education. Early on, she set the tone for educational reform while growing up in North Carolina and employed that passion when she and my dad settled in Teaneck, New Jersey.

In 1964 Teaneck became the first community in America to use busing to voluntarily desegregate its schools. My mom not only embraced that, but was on the front lines of doing even more. She ran a Saturday program teaching African American students the history that wasn't being taught in the schools.

I watched my parents reach out to so many different people to say, "We, as a town, want to commit to not just inclusion as a buzzword, but a real way of life." Watching that, I saw the work that was involved. I saw the benefits. I saw the hope.

That's not to say the incident at camp was the only time a racial slur was thrown at me. When I was ten, I was walking home from school, and a man sitting on his porch called me the N-word, waved a switchblade, and dared me to come over. This was in the town that I extol the virtues of. I thought, *Am I going to die?* I heard similar stuff after high school baseball games when our team played in towns that didn't like Teaneck's diversity.

As time went by Glanville's experiences mirrored those of many people of color—despite the fact that he was at an Ivy League school, that he was a major league baseball player, a familiar face on television. A college teammate worked out draped in a Confederate flag. Other teammates chastised him for wearing a yellow ribbon protesting the expulsion of a black student. A Mercedes dealership ignored him as he looked at the cars on its showroom floor. Cab drivers at airports shunned him.

At some point I realized the "It's not my problem" response I'd had as a five-year-old wasn't the best way to bring people together. I started to understand the power of outreach and being able to engage people you don't necessarily agree with, or who just haven't had the same experience.

He did so in one-to-one and group conversations through op-ed pieces and his book. That philosophy was put to the test in February of 2014. Glanville was shoveling snow in his driveway in Hartford, Connecticut, when a policeman from West Hartford, the next town over, pulled up, got out of his car, and began questioning him. The cop apparently thought Glanville was the "black man in a brown coat" reported to have gone door-to-door in neighboring West Hartford offering to shovel snow. Such solicitation is not a crime, but the exchange with the shoveler led to the police being called after someone identified him at a much later time. Glanville was wearing a black coat, which, to the policeman, was apparently close enough to justify a confrontation at his house.

I was literally standing in my own driveway. It felt like I was robbed, like my security in this space, my home, was being taken. It took a minute to just come down. Why was he there? You have an officer from another town stopping someone across this border and no introduction, no anything. Coming at me demanding to know if I'm shoveling for money. It was absurd, but I just didn't know what to do. I also was thinking about my own safety.

After I established that this was my driveway, the policeman left. No apology. When my wife—a former public defender—returned from a Black History Month event with our kids, she wrote a letter to our neighbor, a state rep. Slowly, supportive neighbors came and we started to form a response, consider some strategies.

One important thing I found in working on these solutions is retaining an open mind. Yes, it was offensive, but I didn't have all the information I needed. Maybe the policeman had been pursuing some gunman. I tried to give him the benefit of the doubt—that it could have been a high stress situation that caused him to skip over certain pleasantries or rules about crossing town lines, which actually did exist.

The first step was understanding. I met with the Hartford chief of police, the West Hartford police, that town's city manager and chair of the board of education. West Hartford is a bedroom community, and many of its residents had been embarrassed to hear what had happened.

After processing all this, I wrote an article for *The Atlantic*, which the editors titled: "I Was Racially Profiled in My Own Driveway." I was more comfortable with the subtitle: "A retired Major League Baseball player explains how he's trying to turn an upsetting encounter with the police into an opportunity for dialogue." I soon received some blowback. Critics said I was overreacting. After all, I hadn't been shot, or even tasered. What was the big deal?

I learned from my parents and from my baseball career to play the long game. I like to quote the character Ragnar Lothbrok from the historical television drama, *Vikings*, who paraphrased the English poet John Dryden in proclaiming: "Never underestimate the fury of a patient man."

When you play that long game, you have to have a certain confidence in justice and believe that your effort is righteous. Unfortunately, it didn't take long for some dominos to fall that persuaded some of my critics that the effort was just. Within months, two unarmed black men died at the hands of police in high profile cases—Michael Brown in Ferguson and Eric Garner in Staten Island.

The months that followed were like an episode of *Schoolhouse Rock*. After much research and numerous meetings with everybody under the sun—the state attorney general's office, councils and committees and officers and lawyers—we determined legislation was the best option. As the bill's sponsor State Rep Mathew Ritter explained: "The objective of the new law is to stop incidents where police officers are crossing town lines for the sole purpose of enforcing a municipal ordinance which carries nothing more than a civil penalty. A police officer should only cross town lines for emergencies, with a warrant or to enforce criminal laws."

I had avoided the media for weeks, but after the bill passed by consent, I broke my silence: "Our country is unquestionably at a crossroads, and I believe the way we were able to legislatively address my experience is an important part of the puzzle. We have seen protests, tears, frustration, collaboration, legislation, sometimes violence and I am glad that I was part of a process that was open, peaceful, strong, and legally sound." Hopefully, by limiting police to working in their own towns where they have a better understanding of the residents and the neighborhoods, we'll be able to avoid high stress encounters that, as we've seen all too often, can escalate with deadly consequences. Just to be on the safe side, I now wear a neon orange coat. I don't want there to be any excuse for being misidentified.

I want to say that I am not an opponent of the police. I had a great youth league coach who was a volunteer policeman. Teammates became officers. Many of my dad's patients were policemen, and when he passed, our family received a police escort from funeral home to cemetery. It was very moving to me personally. Still, when George Floyd was murdered in Minneapolis, I'd had enough and I saw it as an advantage that I could come from a place that showed me how the relationship between law enforcement and police could be positive. My way of engaging in that moment was to write and narrate a video essay that was presented on ESPN and ended up winning an Emmy. It's titled "Enough."

It takes eight minutes and twenty seconds for sunlight to reach the Earth.

In that time, under its warm touch, the world saw George Floyd go cold under the bended knee of injustice and inhumanity.

We stopped, still granted the gift to breathe, trying not to stare, but unable to look away.

Then the tears flowed and the temperature rose.

The glistening streets became thoroughfares of protest until buildings burned under the recklessness of justifiable outrage and hopelessness.

Nothing had changed

We had once again ignored the disinfecting power of the sun.

We had silenced the voices of a people because their peaceful pleas were not made at the right time, at the right place, in the right way.

We were told once again to wait. Even when Martin Luther King Jr. implored us in his *Letter from Birmingham Jail* that "this 'wait' has almost always meant 'never.'"

And the face of smug indifference cast its shadow with self-serving and willful ignorance, defiantly staring into the heart of the sun until we were all blinded by the hate.

Staring with eyes that could see color, but not humanity.

Yet the sun rose again.

To give us another opportunity to be enlightened.

To help us see George Floyd as all of us and not just one of them.

Eight minutes and twenty seconds to realize that we all have the privilege to breathe when others can't.

Enough time to lift a knee.

Enough time to say something.

Enough time to take a deep breath.

Enough time to not send that hateful tweet.

Enough time to ask why I am calling 911.

Enough time to wipe a tear.

Enough time to change a heart.

Enough time to be a teammate.

Enough time to listen.

Enough time to break bread.

Enough time to learn from our differences.

Enough time to raise a flag.

Enough time to pay our respects.

Enough time to love a country.

Enough time to say enough . . . enough.

We have had enough time to change.

But this time, too many times, the light did not illuminate.

Because we shielded our eyes.

From the reflection we did not want to see.

We are eight minutes and twenty seconds too late.

And George Floyd is eternally nonresponsive because we were nonresponsive.

So let's respond and make his death be our light.

When I write on these subjects, I'm calling out injustice. But I'm also framing it—saying, "There's still hope." My criticism is couched in the fact that I see great possibility. I'm not making a conclusion, a final state of affairs here. I'm saying this is a teaching point that we can actually build something on. I think when you see it that way, you bring more people into the solution. And when you bring more people into a solution, whether it's a law, whatever it is, they invest in the outcome, and its future, because there's no solution that's completely elegant.

I've found that the best work is connecting to people, telling stories and communicating all along the way before the outcome. In fact, I'd argue that the engagement up until the final product is actually more important than the final product. It's a long game and it's fighting back against this idea that just because you're black or white that puts you on a side. Even though the dynamics of race are very real, the way I see it, there are no sides. You're trying to center humanity.

FOR MORE INFORMATION:

dougglanville.com

Doug Glanville's book: *The Game from Where I Stand: From Batting Practice to the Clubhouse to the Best Breakfast on the Road, an Inside View of a Ballplayer's Life*, 2011

Doug Glanville's video essay:

https://www.youtube.com/watch?v=WCfoo8LL-NQ

'Art Can Spark Conversation'

CAROLYN CONSIDINE, *18, is a high school senior living in Lafayette, California. While in high school she cofounded two initiatives that further the cause of social justice: Justice Murals and Meaningful Teens.*

I LIVE IN A largely white neighborhood, and my high school is predominantly white. At the beginning of COVID, old videos surfaced of students making racial slurs, saying just horrible things. It actually made national news. My school is very insular to begin with, and I really felt like we needed a way to talk about what was going on and how this was not okay. I wanted to bring people together for a common purpose.

My grandfather is an artist, so I've always had a big love for the arts. I'm Irish and when I was about ten, I went and visited Northern Ireland. We went to see the Peace Walls, which were put up during the Troubles around 1970 to separate the Protestant and Catholic neighborhoods and eventually were painted with these murals that mostly depicted hatred and violence.

I was just shocked and stunned by the art. Our guide called it a "Facebook of sorts" in how it conveys information. But it's also a lot of propaganda. Seeing this I thought, *What would happen if we turned the tables and used art in a positive way as a vehicle for social change and to talk about issues that are going on in our society?* That experience kind of lit the match for my activism.

I feel like today we have all these different social media forums—Facebook, Instagram, TikTok—but I think we're kind of losing this idea of a public square. People may post news about issues, but there's no real common area where they are talking about them. We have all these digital public squares, which is great, but when you have a thousand of them, it's not a public square anymore.

When I saw those disgusting videos combined with all the social injustice that was happening—George Floyd and other things—it reminded me of Northern Ireland and how it may have physical walls, but we have these more invisible social walls that go back hundreds of years and are still here. And I thought it was really time to bring them down and talk about it and open up these conversations.

I've always loved how art can spark conversations and impact people. I am part of this group for my county, AC5—the Contra Costa County Arts and Culture Commission. I'm the only young person on the commission. I'm on it because I just put myself out there and applied. It's a lovely group of adults, and they're really my mentors. I'm always having conversations with them, asking, "What do you think of this idea?" I do a lot of work for the group, setting up art galleries and showcasing student art, which around the time of those videos was focused on social justice. So that's where the idea of justice murals came to me.

I talked with my AC5 group about it, my advisor at school Mr. Turner, and my vice-principal, and they all thought it was a good idea. So we sent out an email asking students to submit drawings and words of what social justice means to them. Then I worked with a team of artists from the community, and we took all of these words and drawings and ideas together to make a cohesive mural. It's great because you can have hundreds of kids involved in this process. They're the artists, which is really wonderful.

We hung the murals in the school in areas of prominence that people often walk by. It was a great way to bring the community back together after what had happened in the videos and move the conversation beyond the Diversity, Equality, and Inclusion classes we have at school. Since Justice Murals started in 2020, it has spread to twenty-five schools.

We've also partnered with ArtLords, which describes itself as a "global art for social transformation movement." It was started by Omaid Sharifi, an Afghan muralist. He's painted over two thousand murals in Kabul. When the Taliban came in, they painted over all of his murals; the art was that powerful. I heard about it on the news and reached out to him and he responded, which was very exciting.

I've been working with him ever since, doing projection artwork—where I go to immigrant communities and do a popup and then project some of his art on a wall. People sometimes come up to me and say they're from Afghanistan and they've seen his art in their hometown.

Besides Justice Murals, I also cofounded Meaningful Teens, which is a nonprofit where we teach literacy and English to low-income and immigrant children. It grew out of the fact that in eighth grade, my good friend Isabella and I were volunteering at a low-income senior facility in Walnut Creek. When Covid started, we wanted to continue, so we started meeting over Zoom with breakout rooms. It opened a lot of opportunities and allowed me to help more people than I could just help by myself. That gave us the idea of tutoring kindergarten-age kids over Zoom.

Meaningful Teens started with just the two of us, but then we put out the word to friends and it spread. We now have over eight hundred twenty online volunteer tutors working with hundreds of kids. We've added credentialed teachers that kind of hop into all the different breakout rooms and check in and see how everything's going.

They can see certain things. Sometimes, they'll say, "This child might have dyslexia," or, "This student needs glasses," and we're able to set them up and get them glasses or whatever they need, which especially at that age is very important.

The literacy rates of these kindergartners have grown from zero to 70 percent, twice the rate of kids who aren't in the program. Now we're doing different projects in a number of schools and working with older kids and seniors, too. We also give books away to kids and sponsor talks and conversations about diversity and volunteering.

We're teaching literacy, but we're also helping these kids feel so much more confident in themselves and their reading abilities. That, I think, is the biggest thing you can give a kid.

What I really love about Justice Murals and Meaningful Teens is that we inspire youth and other students to be the leaders. Sometimes for Meaningful Teens, we'll have a student who wants to run their own program, helping kids in India, for example. Or they're really interested in music and they want to do something with teaching music and literacy to kids combined. I'll say, "Great, great. Do the program. Let's make it happen." Once you say "yes" to a student, so many doors open and so many possibilities happen.

I now have a position on the public art committee for my town of Lafayette. I think the most important part of activism is listening to others. So often people are quick to speak for others without hearing what they have to say. I think in order to have these conversations, we need a round table and we need everyone's voices to be heard. We need to be active listeners. Empathy and human compassion and kindness for others are such basic things, but so often they're overlooked and not used.

One of my mentors always ends her emails to me with the quote: "And go." That's the best advice I can give. Don't be afraid to fight for social justice. It can seem scary, but it's not in a lot of ways. Don't feel that your age is a negative thing. I often think it's a positive thing to be young. People want to hear the youth perspective.

Once you do get involved, you have to accept that not everything is perfect; there will be bumps. Sometimes something happens and you just have to go with it. One time we ended up with a mural that was printed in the wrong way, and I had to fix it. Things pop up. But the upside is just so much greater than the downside.

Teenagers and young adults really can make a huge impact and create huge changes and continue these conversations that we're having. It really comes down to having a *we*, not *me*, mentality of how together we can create something much more beautiful. It's a better outcome when we work together than when we work alone.

I have gotten some pushback on social media—crazy comments from people on Facebook. But that doesn't stop me, and I really hope that doesn't stop other people from wanting to be involved and wanting to talk about these issues. I think by being silent and not talking about them, you're almost continuing the problems in a way. I mean, as people say, *silence is violence*. You're just keeping things as they are.

And so I think it's almost a social responsibility for us—the next generation. We're the ones that have to change society and fix issues. And if we don't speak up, if we don't talk about it, then, gosh, why are we here? If things stay the same, it's not just. Society should always be progressing and improving. As humans, that's what we should strive to do.

I can understand how social media trolls and negative things like that can scare people. But don't listen to that noise of people trying to bring you down and stop you. Put that in a box and put it in the trash and keep these conversations going. Put yourself out there, send that email, put yourself in an awkward situation. The worst-case scenario is you get a "no." But the "yes" so outweighs the "no."

FOR MORE INFORMATION:
www.justicemurals.org
www.meaningfulteens.org
www.artlords.co

'Posting in Earnest'

ERYNN CHAMBERS, *30, is an educator and social media creator from Kings Mountain, North Carolina. In 2021,* USA Today *described her as "one of the most important creators raising awareness of the black experience and racism on TikTok." She is followed by almost one million viewers, and her work has received almost one hundred million "likes."*

THE GEORGE FLOYD MURDER was a major turning point for me. I was on TikTok at the time and becoming more aware of certain issues because of the people I was following. That's actually where I first saw the George Floyd video. That, combined with my exposure to a lot of different causes and activist content on TikTok, led me from just watching things to making things. I started to make videos about subjects that were interesting to me, such as linguistics and social justice. Eventually social justice became a running theme.

I was homeschooled in a pretty religious conservative home in Gastonia, North Carolina. My mom did most of my teaching and made sure to talk about slavery and the effects of racism. I was aware of the civil rights movement, but I don't think I really realized how important race discussions are until I got a little older.

I was raised in a southern conservative town, surrounded by white people for the most part. That was part of the reason that it took me a lot longer than most to realize the impact of systemic racism. I thought if I just assimilated to the white culture I was surrounded by, I would be safe. I graduated from a PWI (Primarily White Institution) in 2016.

I was probably about twenty-five when I started paying closer attention to social justice issues.

I started listening to the people who were talking about Black Lives Matter and what their grievances were and started paying more attention to things like police brutality and other inequalities and realizing that it was worse than I had realized. Because, you know, there's two Americas, and I didn't realize that necessarily until I was a little bit older and really spoke to people from different experiences.

I had some racist encounters as a kid. I remember when I was around four years old, I was in a ballet class and there was a little white girl who refused to hold my hand because I was black. But I didn't have too many overtly racist experiences like that. I think I was more forgiving than I really needed to be just because I was surrounded by white people, and micro-aggressions were common.

I started teaching when I was twenty-five. I teach music in an elementary school here in North Carolina. My classes are about two-thirds white, with the other third being black and Hispanic. I make an effort to create a discussion or awareness of cultural issues. For example, there's this hip hop string duo called Black Violin—twin black brothers who are classically trained musicians. I show their videos to my students a lot. One time when we were talking about stringed instruments, I showed a video of theirs where they were playing "Lift Every Voice and Sing," and it was set off against pictures of the George Floyd protest. So that was a good, easy way to expose my students to what was happening and allow them to hear that song in a civil rights context.

For Black History Month, I'll often incorporate stories of jazz and the history of jazz and blues and some of the greats and the prejudice that they faced. There's a children's story about Ella Fitzgerald and her friendship with Marilyn Monroe and how Marilyn Monroe helped her perform at a club that had been discriminating. It's written in plain language, easy for children to understand, and can lead to a discussion of what that looked and felt like.

According to Tiktok, as of 2022, I have about 860,000 followers and over ninety-one million "likes "to my posts. My audience skews younger, but I definitely have older followers as well. Using the name Rynnstar, I started posting in earnest during the Covid quarantine in 2020. A country western parody I did went viral and then so did a video I did shortly after the George Floyd murder, labeled, "About y'alls favorite 'statistics.'"

The lyrics I wrote and sang were simple: and the video received two million views.

> Black neighborhoods are over-policed, so of course they have higher rates of crime. And white perpetrators are undercharged, so of course they have lower rates of crime. And all those stupid stats that you keep using are operating off a small sample size. So shut up, shut up, shut up, shut up, shut up, shut up, shut up.

TikTok to me was different from any other social media platform in terms of what it exposed me to. I was on Tumblr before that—actually on the conservative side of Tumblr—and so I was mostly surrounded by like-minded people. But on TikTok, you have this face to face. I had never really interacted with Native Americans before I became "mutuals" with them on TikTok. I learned a lot more about their issues.

TikTok is unique in that the people who create on there are just individuals from different experiences and walks of life. And you get an intimate look into their lived experience in a way that just reading about it doesn't give you.

I post about pretty much whatever catches my fancy that day. Sometimes I'm reading up on something and want to share what I've learned. Sometimes I'm wanting to give somebody a deeper perspective into historical characters they may not know much about. For example, I made a video labeled, "Why is Rosa Parks the only black activist we learn about?" I talked about her predecessor, Claudette Colvin, who most people have never heard of. So I'm giving people a new perspective on the history that they were taught in school.

TikTok provides a way to kind of distill information down into a very manageable package and give people a sort of a flyover understanding of certain things. I think that that can be very effective when it comes to education. I wouldn't use TikTok exclusively for research, but I think that it is definitely a great starting point.

It can actually explain things to people who are up in arms about certain issues. For example, a lot of people were rallying against the idea of critical race theory because their favorite politicians or whoever told them they ought to be against it. But they have no idea what it even is. With TikTok, a lot of times you can meet people where they're at and actually talk about why you believe this or why you disagree with that. You can say, "Here's my perspective," and sometimes you can get through to people that way.

The fact is that because a lot of the attention span is waning, social media is a way to get people hooked and wanting to learn more. You have to be able to communicate succinctly. If you get people passionate enough about something, they'll be willing to devote a little more time to considering what you're fighting for.

I would define activism as striving to make change in a meaningful way, by getting the word out, getting information out, and really insisting on that change and whatever means that might be required. You know, we do peaceful marches and stuff like that, and that's good. But sometimes things have had to be taken by force as well. I think that it's a matter of being relentless with it. Not giving up and letting those in power feel like they've worn you down.

Sometimes I'm amazed how many people are willing and interested in tuning into what I have to say. And I do feel honored and privileged and blessed to be able to provide that for people who might not otherwise have as much access to it.

I hope someday to move into the field of either journalism or law or something in that regard and be able to make a difference in people's lives, standing up for what I believe.

FOR MORE INFORMATION:
TikTok: Rynnstar
Twitter: TheRealRynnstar
Instagram: TheRealRynnstar
Website: Wordytalk.com
Youtube: Wordy and Nerdy
Podcast: Hot Tea, Hot Takes

'A Safe Space for Native Youth'

ANTHONY TAMEZ-POCHEL, *23, is a neighborhood services coordinator with the City of Chicago, a member of the Chi-Nations Youth Council, and chairman of the Youth Advisory Board of the Center for Native American Youth.*

WITH THE HELP OF our aunts, we threw one of the largest protests in the Midwest because of what was happening up in Canada, with the pipeline companies and the Canadian government infringing on Indigenous rights and Indigenous sovereignty. We were all children; I would say like twelve or thirteen.

At that point in my life, I had already started asking myself: Why are Native people constantly being pushed around? On our own land! Why is it that the government can make treaties with us and then say, "Oh, we don't want to honor this treaty"—and Native people have absolutely no power to say "no."

That's not to say we don't say "no," because we do, and we're constantly fighting. But there's just larger forces that can come in and bully us. At that moment, in getting ready for that protest, I thought, *Enough is enough.*

My activism comes from my family. I grew up in a Native household in Chicago, raised by my aunties and my mom—no father—who were always activists. They've told me stories about taking me to protests when I was a baby. They taught me how to march, instructed me in civil disobedience.

A Native household is a multi-generational home where everyone is living together and taking care of each other. I've never not lived with my cousins or my aunties. In my culture we call our aunties on my mother's side our moms. So I have four moms. Just sitting down in the living room, listening to them talk about their experiences and what they go through every day as Native women has really influenced me.

I'm black *and* Native—First Nations Cree and Sicangu Lakota. People treat me differently because of the curl in my hair and the color of my skin. For the longest time I would make excuses, say racism isn't the reason. But deep down I think I understood some of the reasons behind things that were said to me or the way people acted towards me

My first protest, as far as I can recall, was the NATO demonstration in Chicago in 2012. My aunts had already gone the previous days, and everything had been tense for some days. I was just eleven years old at the time, and our visit was nothing like anything they had previously encountered. It was more laid-back. However, I recall being overjoyed that I was able to march in the street with my aunts.

The next year other Native kids in Chicago and I observed protests against the pipeline taking place around the country and said, "We want to participate in this and express our support." Our aunts showed us how to organize it, which took a few weeks.

Native people who weren't even from Chicago showed up. We were in the front of the line leading them through downtown Chicago. We didn't get a permit. As Native people, we're adamant about the fact that we're not going to get a permit to march on our own land. It's kind of similar to where you used to need permits to go out on the Chicago River in your canoes. And we're like, "I'm not going to pay you to do something we have traditionally done."

At the protest, Native youth were able to speak. It was my first time speaking in front of a huge crowd. I recall thinking, *Holy crap, this place is packed*! I was worried beforehand, but I remember that once up there simply feeling so passionate about what I was saying and hearing people applaud. *Wow.* They were interested in what a small brown boy had to say! It gave me the sense that what I say matters.

I realized this is what my life is going to be: fighting for rights of Indigenous people and the liberation of black people. At the same time, I remember feeling: *This isn't fair. Why is it that I constantly have to do this? Why can't I just grow up and walk through life without a care in the world?* That's not my way of thinking now. It's more: *Okay, this is the work that needs to get done. We're gonna get it done.*

About this time, the Chi-Nations Youth Council was formed. Our mission is to create a safe space for Native youth through arts, activism, and education. We do a lot of environmental work, connecting the residents of the City of Chicago to the land that they're living on. Over the years, among other things, we've created a First Nations community garden; participated in the removal of the Columbus statues in Chicago; addressed anti-blackness in the Indian community; and worked for the removal of race-based mascots, including the Chicago Blackhawks logo, which to us symbolize a legacy of imperialism and genocide.

Some friends ask me why these logos are bad. I explain they are always from the neck up—an area where they would cut Native people's heads off or scalp them, put them on stakes. And I point to work by psychologists like Dr. Stephanie Fryberg, whose studies show the very real harmful effects they have on Native children because they remind them of the limited ways in which others see us.

I had the opportunity to talk with elected officials about this issue a few years ago when I was chosen to be a Champion for Change at the Center for Native American Youth at the Aspen Institute. Each year the Center selects five "up and coming Native American change-makers" between the age of fourteen and twenty-three. They flew us to Washington, D.C., and I was able to tell Illinois Senators Durbin and Duckworth and Congressman Mike Quigley about the work I was doing.

They were all very nice and said to keep up the great work, but I saw that they had a lack of knowledge of Native people. And in Chicago we have one of the largest populations of Native people in the country.

So I thought, *Okay we need Native people in government. We need our own people in there to think about us so we can continue to fight for our cultural and beliefs and rights.*

Since 2018, I've actually worked in government for the City of Chicago. For most of that time, I've worked as a Neighborhood Service Coordinator for a progressive alderperson, working on ordinances, community-driven zoning, and a number of projects with both local businesses and youth. That's how we were able to get access to the five plots of land that make up our First Nations Garden.

I see how our government was built on and is based on anti-Indian policies and that when we talk about our city's history, we don't talk about the Native people that were here. We have essentially erased the fact that the first person here was a Haitian man who married a Potawatomi woman and became part of that tribe.

Some of this is due to downright prejudice. I've heard people say, "We killed your people off. Why are you here? Why are you speaking?" Essentially, "Why don't you go off into the corner and be quiet."

But I would say the majority of this is out of ignorance. A lot of people don't understand how their actions have been harmful to indigenous people or blacks. Being able to sit down with them and explain why often ends up with them saying, "Oh, I didn't even realize that."

Having been involved in protests against the government, I get some pushback for working in government. But there are different types of activism, right? There are people like myself who work from inside the system. There are people who work outside of the system, like nonprofits, foundations. There are agitators. All are very important parts to a movement.

I understand that working in government there are things that you cannot do. I was very young when I was hired, nineteen—still going through school—and I already knew Native people do not have the best relationship with government from federal down to city. I want to do good in this space, but I know that in order for me to do the good that I want to do, there is without a doubt harm that happens in the process. I know that in getting from point A to point B there are going to be times where I either do things that are harmful to my own community or harmful to other communities, and I have to be very open and transparent about that and be willing to be held accountable for whatever I may have done.

Working for a local government or any government at all, I think it's pretty safe to say that we know the types of people that the government works for and works against. So being in these positions, you are sometimes working against your own people, but you're also trying to work *for* your own people. You are trying to walk this very thin line of how can we make the best of the situation.

I've simply come to the realization that I would much rather have someone who looks like me and has my values in government. I'm fortunate that the alderperson I worked for, unlike her predecessors, believes government should treat its citizens properly.

One of the specific things that I like to bring up to explain why it's so necessary for people like myself to be in these positions deals with homelessness. We have a fair amount of homeless people living in our ward. With the past alderpersons, the neighbors would call and say, "I want this person removed." And the alderperson would call the police and the homeless person would get arrested for doing something like sleeping on a bench. They'd be held, then released, and they'd come right back. That's not fixing something.

But the process we now have set up calls family and support services instead of the police to see what kind of actual services they need. Do they need help relocating to a place that's safer for them? It's those reasons why it's necessary for people like me to be there.

I continue to practice my culture. It teaches us to leave this world or place better than when we came into it. And I've seen how some of the work that I've done in my community is already benefiting some of the Native youth here. That's something that keeps me going.

One of my hopes is that the work I'm doing is for something seven generations from now. They're not going to have to think about the same things I'm having to think about. That's a very Native way of thinking as well, thinking seven generations, because my ancestors seven generations ago thought about their actions and how it was going to impact Native people in the future.

What keeps me going is not the thinking, *Oh, this isn't fair.* It's the mindset that the work needs to get done. We're gonna get it done. And we're gonna get it done through any means necessary.

FOR MORE INFORMATION:
chinations.org

'He's Captain America'

VISHAVJIT SINGH, 51, is a cartoonist, writer, performance artist, and the creator of Sikhtoons.com based in New York City. He is a public speaker expounding on diversity, inclusion, storytelling and the power of art in schools, universities, and companies across the nation

AND THEN, SEPTEMBER 11 happened. That terrible attack on my country was quickly followed by attacks on people who looked like me. I worked from home for the next two weeks. But I couldn't avoid the hostility. Never before had so many strangers been compelled to call me names: Osama, Taliban, Raghead, Towelhead.

The first victim of a hate crime after the attacks was a Sikh in Arizona. In the aftermath, I was struck by an animated cartoon by Pulitzer Prize winner Mark Fiore that appeared online with the title, "Find the Terrorist." The sequence featured a Sikh man, a Hindu man, a Muslim, a Latino and a white man. You had to click on the rotating images to find out who the terrorist was. With each click you got introduced to each character. Joe, the white man having committed a hate crime against the Muslim man, was the terrorist. It's such a simple thing. It's a cartoon, but it had a character who looked like me. Mark captured the predicament of brown and Sikh Americans.

I moved with my Sikh family from Washington, D.C., to New Delhi, India, in early adolescence. I grew up watching Bollywood movies, where Sikhs like me were always punch lines of the jokes. In 1984, Indian Prime Minister Indira Gandhi was shot dead by two of her Sikh bodyguards, and for the next few days the country erupted in mayhem. Sikhs were hunted down and burned alive. After high school

I left India and headed back to the United States, a place that I hoped might be more tolerant, but out on the streets young and old would pass me by and burst into laughter.

When I arrived at Ohio State University, my bright blue turban still made me the center of attention, but I was more like an exotic specimen. It was a relief. But then the first Iraq war began. Even though the turban was not worn by any of the Iraqi forces, it became a visual cue for hate. More than a few fellow Americans told me, "Go back home."

I left the Midwest for the University of California—Santa Barbara and better times. The war was over and I was accepted with open arms by a much more diverse community. Ironically, in the midst of this acceptance, I decided—after years of taunts and hate—I didn't want to stand out anymore. I cut my hair for the first time in twenty years and abandoned my turban. I moved away from my religion and tried to find my professional passion. I focused on epidemiology and biostatistics and dabbled in Taoism and Buddhism.

When I moved in for a time with my brother during graduate school, I couldn't escape my heritage. He played hymns from the Sikh scriptures on his stereo 24/7. It felt strangely foreign, but by the time I concluded my master's program, I had fallen in love with kirtan from the Sikh scriptures, poetic verses sung in adoration of the divine.

Those verses and the many books I read during this time saved me. The three authors who influenced me most were Studs Terkel, Oliver Sacks, and Elie Wiesel. Of course, they are all very different, but they are all great storytellers and all full of compassion.

When I moved back east, not far from New York City, I embraced my faith. By August 2001, I had my waist-length hair back. I tied it in a bun on top of my head, which served as an anchor for my six-foot-long blue turban.

And then, as I said, 9/11 happened. And after that, the cartoon, which so brilliantly captured the truth as it was playing out on the streets. Fiore exhibited a rare courage in publicly labeling the crimes being committed against Muslims and anyone else perceived as a Muslim. These were acts of terrorism.

That emotional moment provided a creative spark for me to start envisioning Sikhs in the world of editorial cartoons. I finally discovered the best way to respond to a lifetime of being a target of hate, living with it, and even accepting it. I raised my right index finger, moved it across the tiny computer touch pad and began to capture the world of Sikhs here at home and around the globe in cartoons.

I kept my day job as a software engineer. But, thanks to the internet, this unknown cartoonist developed a global following. As I put my work out there on my website, Sikhtoons.com, I started hearing from people. Teachers from across the country started reaching out to me, saying, "We'd love to have you come to our school."

For the next several years, I hosted storytelling sessions in schools, but my cartooning was still a side job. Then, at the suggestion of some friends, I went to the 2011 New York Comic Con as an exhibitor. That was the same year the first *Captain America* movie came out. I dream in turban and beards, and as I was preparing for this trip. I had this vision: *I'm gonna create something fresh to attract people to my booth* And so I sketched Captain America with a turban and beard. *This Captain America is going to fight hate and intolerance—the biggest villains in America for a long time.*

So I took this poster with me, not knowing how people were going to respond. Some people got it. Others didn't. "Why is Captain America a Muslim?" they asked. It started these conversations, and I realized, *Wow, something's going on here.*

Fiona Aboud, a photographer who was working on a photo essay about Sikhs in America, came by, saw the poster, and said, "Hey, that's really cool. Maybe next year you should come dressed up as Captain America." I said no. But then ten months later in 2012, there was a massacre at a Sikh house of worship in Milwaukee. I wrote an op-ed presenting the case that we needed a new comic superhero in America. Fiona read it and encouraged me to reconsider my decision to dress up as Captain America for a photo shoot on the streets of New York City. She said, "Let's push people's perceptions of what it means to be American."

I did it, thinking it would be a one-time thing, but it was like we entered a parallel universe where people treated me so differently—in a good way. They saw me dressed up as Captain America: skinny, glasses, turban, beard. And they thought, *Wow, this guy is one of our own. He's Captain America!*

Following the photo shoot, I wrote an op-ed for *Salon*, releasing a few photos. The story and photos went viral. And I realized: *I'm going to be a performance artist and a storyteller. I'm going to go on this journey.*

I've been on the road since then with people inviting me into their companies, schools, not-for-profits, even government agencies. Five or six years ago, I finally said, "Okay, this is my passion." I transitioned out of my job. And I've been doing public speaking ever since.

When I speak to kids, I use my cartoons to tell my story of somebody who was born in the U.S. Somebody who's had identity struggles, who's been bullied and abused. Then I connect issues of race and bias and prejudice and vulnerability. I end with my Captain America performance art. Basically, I use my story as a lens to talk about broader issues like bias and racism.

One piece of wisdom I have learned over time is: what we have in common is our prejudices towards other human beings. It's just how we have evolved. And maybe we can use that as a starting point to have conversations, because we tend to typically say, "I don't have prejudices." Let's talk about what prejudices we all have. And it starts genuine connections.

I find my most powerful presentations happen in schools because kids are very honest and transparent. I start by asking people the question, "What comes to mind when you see me? Where do you think I'm from?" Most place me outside of the U.S., but by the time I'm done with my story, I ask the question again, and now they use words like cool, creative, courageous, brave, honest, and artistic.

That's the message I want to leave with everyone. "Look, you didn't know me. You let your brain and stereotypes judge me. You know a little bit of my story now. And now you see me radically differently. If we created a world where we could all share our stories, a little bit, we'd have a hard time judging each other just based on what our eyes see."

I have a profound respect for the wisdom we have as young children, but we don't allow kids to just be who they are and, in a sense, learn from them. Kids are transparent. They ask questions, but the way they ask questions is not offensive. One of the most important things we can do to transform societies is to start very early on in our schools and homes and be very comfortable talking about our vulnerabilities. Courage comes out of our vulnerabilities.

After my talk I do interactive sessions where the students create art based on their stories and imaginations. Sometimes they come up to me and say, "Thank you for sharing your story. I've struggled with these things. I've struggled with mental health." Or: "I've had this challenge in my family."

The only people in this world who give me hope for the future are the young kids. We're handing them a pretty messy world. They're better equipped than my generation to deal with the messiness we're handing over to them.

With the adults who host me, I ask the same questions. "Where do you think I'm from?" It's not that different from kiddos. And then I share my story again, using my cartoons with lots of turban and bearded characters, and then I get into race. I'm honest about my own prejudices. I explain that the goal here is to become better versions of who we are as individuals and as societal institutions. And the only way you can do that is by acknowledging problems you have. Because if you don't have any problems, well, we don't have much to talk about to change.

I started a journey of becoming a cartoonist. And now I'm a performance artist dressed as Captain America, a writer, and a public speaker. I've found an artistic outlet to build bridges with people. That's my activism: telling my story in a world where we don't know each other's stories and construct imaginary differences. And using my skills to help other people tell their stories.

Of course, I wish 9/11 had never happened. But tragedies happen. It's what you do with tragedies that is so critical. You can get really angry. I was upset. Fortunately I found cartooning as a way to channel my frustration and anger and to find connections with people who misjudge and misperceive me.

The key is being transparent, honest with yourself. Let your vulnerabilities do the talking. We're told: "Focus only on the good parts. Don't reveal too much." But I have learned over time that if you want to become a better version of yourself, just let it out, just share with people what you've gone through. Once you open that door, you're going to find courage to do things that you need to do.

I cannot emphasize enough the importance of reading, because you will find characters in books who are going through what you're going through.

Find your voice. Become an advocate for yourself and others. Say, "I'm gonna change this." It has changed in the past. The arc is bending in the right direction, but sometimes we take a few steps backward.

All of us have the potential to be advocates and leaders. If you're going through a difficult time, don't run away from it. Use that as your channel towards becoming a changemaker for the better,

The most powerful superpowers we all possess are compassion, kindness, perseverance and patience. If you read stories of people that have changed the world, you'll see it takes many years, sometimes multiple lifetimes. The key is dropping seeds. Trees don't grow in a single day. The key is not necessarily getting to your destination tomorrow. The key is learning every day.

FOR MORE INFORMATION:
Sikhtoons.com

'Fighting Racism'

BEN SHORE, 22, *and* DEONTE HANNAH, 23, *are cofounders and directors of the Cherry Hills, New Jersey–based Rise Against Hate (RAH). Created in 2020, this nonprofit raises awareness about racism and civil rights. Ben is a student at American University in Washington, D.C. DeOnte is in business.*

BEN: After George Floyd was murdered in May of 2020, I was driving and I started crying because I was so disappointed in what our world has become. I pulled off to the side of the road to process everything and started thinking about how my experience is different than some of my cousins who are black.

While I was parked there, a cop actually came behind me to check on me. And I had this second flash where, I thought: *Wow, if I was somebody else—if I wasn't white—I might have been fearing that I could get shot by the policeman who had pulled up.* It really made me wake up.

My first effort was as a first grader. I went to each student and petitioned for more balls at recess, and we got another basketball. Growing up as an individual with a disability (I'm on the autism spectrum), I really needed to advocate to get the accommodations that I needed to be successful—especially in school. I learned the importance of allyship and of helping others.

Both my uncles are black and I have several black cousins. One of my uncles has been pulled over so many times. Hearing about this discrimination, learning good values from my parents, reading about John Lewis, encourages me to stand up against hate.

DeOnte: My definition of activism is people coming together to fight for one belief, to stand up for one cause, to make a big positive change in a community.

Ben: Before DeOnte and I started Rise Against Hate, I took on a variety of causes. When I was sixteen, I went city to city in New Jersey, fighting for civil rights, essentially using the Constitution to strike down an order that disproportionately affected people of color. The following year, I passed my first civil rights legislation into law. I believe if you see something that impacts a certain category of people, then you need to make change.

DeOnte: My experience is different. As an African American teenager, watching the news and seeing things—I don't want to say, racist—but seeing things like the close-mindedness of this generation, is what pushed me to become more active.

Ben: DeOnte and I met at the Jersey Shore and became friends. And within a few weeks of the George Floyd murder, we said it's time to stand up, time to take some action. We formulated some ideas and launched Rise against Hate.

DeOnte: I've always wanted to step ahead, to lead, to be my own person. In our conversations, I realized this is bigger than just me. This is bigger than just Ben. This is bigger than just our neighbors. This is about the country realizing what everybody's going through. There's no voice for the people. So when Ben brought the idea up, I thought, *Why not*? Because we need somebody who's at the bottom willing to say, "This is what we go through. This is what we see every day that y'all don't know about."

Ben: One of the first things with RAH was to create a mission statement, which right now is "raise awareness about racism and civil rights, investigate racial disparities, and provide public awareness in law." One example of that is we helped pass the law in New Jersey establishing the Amistad Commission Exemplary Award Program, which honors educators who have shown a commitment to furthering student knowledge on slavery in America, the vestiges of slavery in the U.S., and the contributions of African Americans to our society.

I have a paralegal certificate, so I was able to do the paperwork necessary to establish Rise Against Hate as a not-for-profit. While we were waiting for that to come through, we were able to establish a board with some of the best and brightest minds to help us accomplish our mission. We put up some links on Facebook asking, "Would you like to get involved in making the world a more equitable place?" Within days we had dozens of people just asking to join the team from every field—lawyers, doctors, professors, teachers, psychologists, clergy, students, and more. Getting our mission statement just right was important so it would resonate with people wanting to make an impact. We now have over fifty board members.

We also created a website. You have to give that as much thought as your mission statement. When people come to a website, you might have 30 seconds to get their attention. We put out our mission statement, the studies, who we are, and the important resources we offer. That way you can find out exactly what we are from the moment you get to our site.

DeOnte: It's the same with social media. You have to think: *How can I get them to even stop and read the post?* Anybody can be on social media. Anybody can be scrolling. So presentation is everything. The design, the font, the graphic. All that plays a part into how we grab the attention of our targets.

Ben: If you go to our website now, you can see what we've been able to do in a short time: things like producing a comprehensive study on police use of force and arrests for Cherry Hill Township and creating a RAH Bias program. That was done by two doctors from the University of Pennsylvania. We've created an internship program that gives students opportunities in many fields, and we have a section with resources for fighting racism. We also worked with my aunt Jessica Shore, a psychologist who had been at University of Pennsylvania, to create the nonprofit Nava Center, which treats racial trauma. She's a director on our board, and I'm on her board.

I want to also say that RAH is different than a lot of nonprofits in that we are self-sustaining. We're supported by government and online grants. We are powered by Google, and we qualify for $120,000 from them. Like the American Red Cross and some other nonprofits, we've also been able to increase the amount of money coming in by accepting donations in cryptocurrency.

There are a lot of problems that need to be addressed. One part of our approach is to ask: "What can we win?" For example, we filed lawsuits on behalf of children with disabilities and won or settled every one of them.

We also ask: "How much does it cost? Can we reasonably get it done? And what would the equitable result be? Are we going to help ten people, ten thousand people, one million people? What are we capable of? How can we help?" And then we ask, "Who would be the best person to help accomplish the goal?"

DEONTE: My favorite thing that we have done so far is trying to help the Cherry Hill police think about how they interact with people, especially when it comes to somebody of a different ethnic group. Our mission is goal-oriented, to make sure the police know how to proceed fairly with particular groups of people, groups who might get stopped in their cars or on the street.

If you find the right people, say in a police department, they'll be willing to listen to anything you say if you present yourself the right way. They'll be willing to listen with an open mind, open ears, on what you're trying to do.

BEN: I am still a student at American University in Washington, D.C. I plan on being a student for life, spending a lifetime of education to continue to further develop my skills, and then practice law.

If you start something like RAH that leads to success, there's definitely room to grow. At this point we've been 100 percent volunteer-based and we've been doing that pretty well. It seems that every single day we continue to get more volunteer applications.

DeONTE: I am a man of many things. I'm an independent contractor, and I also work for a nationwide company. I'm trying to move up the rungs. Hopefully, I can bring some of the things I learned from Rise Against Hate into that company, too.

I have three pieces of advice to give to young people like Ben and me who want to solve problems in society. My first would be to stop and think about what's going on, what you can bring to the situation, hopefully not anything negative that would make the situation work worse.

My second thing would be to make sure that if you do speak out about the situation, that you're doing it in the best way possible for yourself and for those around you—that you're not escalating a situation. The whole point is to bring passion to things that nobody else wants to do.

And third, build with a clear heart and a clear voice. You can set that example that we need to change, and we will not tolerate this

BEN: My three tips to somebody who wants to make a difference would be: First, when you feel something is not right or is unjust, recognize it. Maybe not everybody will see it, but if you see it, you feel it, and you know there's something wrong with it, don't be afraid to take action.

My second tip is to be persistent. Change does not happen overnight. You have to be willing to put the work into it, to follow up three, maybe four times. Sometimes elected officials might take a few extra emails to respond, especially to emails about the topics they do not wants to get into.

And then third and most importantly, find coalition partners. Find people who have like-minded views as yours. Find people who are fighting for the causes like yours and team up. I can't overestimate the power of a team. For example, when we went in with the NAACP president of Camden County in New Jersey to talk with a police chief, it really stepped up the game—because now there's a second level of accountability. So find your partners, find your community collaborators.

FOR MORE INFORMATION:

riseagainsthate.org

'Photography with Intention'

SEBASTIÁN HIDALGO, *27, is an independent visual journalist, teaching artist, writer, and National Geographic Explorer. Raised and later displaced from his Chicago neighborhood of Pilsen, he often examines the meaning of belonging in his work. He covers and studies immigration, low-wage labor, housing, and environmental injustices.*

I DISCOVERED PHOTOGRAPHY IN Mexico. I grew up in Pilsen with a single mom, so when her father, my grandfather, was in hospice in Mexico, she brought me with her to help take care of him. I was in the same room during his passing, and it had a profound impact on me. Not in a way that was traumatic or sad. Obviously that moment has intense emotions in it. But it was also such an affirmation to live life. To love life. I was eleven or twelve at the time, and he taught me in those last moments what I had to do moving forward.

While we were there, my uncle tasked me with the duty of photographing everything. He wanted time to mourn the passing of his father, so he gave me a camera he had brought from Chicago and said, "Go nuts with it."

I wanted to communicate what I saw to my two older brothers who weren't there. It was really important to try to document this factual thing, which was seven goodbye kisses to seven children and wife. I realized that this camera, this tool, was extremely important to try to communicate so that others would see the lessons for themselves and make their own judgments.

Pilsen is a small neighborhood a couple of miles south and west of downtown Chicago. There's a lot of history there when it comes to the Mexican experience in the Midwest. Along with Little Village, a neighborhood right next door, and Cicero, the neighboring suburb, Pilsen encompasses what is usually referred to as the Mexican Mecca of the Midwest—a gateway for migrant families to work in the city's factories and other businesses.

When I came back from Mexico, I realized photography was the thing that I needed to do, the craft that I needed to communicate with, a way for me to really understand where I was in the world. I asked my mother for a camera and we got a twenty-dollar Minolta XGM with a 50 millimeter lens.

Photography became my main method of communication. I would purposefully get lost in the neighborhood taking pictures. I think the elders liked seeing a youthful person dive into something creative. I would take pictures of gang graffiti or people on their porches. I was just photographing what I knew, unaware that it was probably one of the most important periods of Pilsen—with the neighborhood changing.

In high school I took a few photography classes, but I really just taught myself by kind of experimenting. By the time I graduated, I knew I wanted to be a photojournalist. That came from a primary instinct to get closer to people. I took a quote from Robert Capa to heart: "If your pictures aren't good enough, you're not close enough."

Not literally. I took it metaphorically, that he was talking about establishing intimate relationships with the people you want to photograph. I saw the worth in documenting those moments that changed my life or other people's lives similarly to the moment I shared with my grandfather.

I started freelancing right away—going into neighborhoods that others wouldn't necessarily want to go to after a certain part of the day. Having grown up in an environment where hyper vigilance is the lesson you need to learn, I was comfortable going to a neighborhood after 6:30 at night and talking to folks that I could relate to. I wanted to try to encompass a lot of information into one particular photograph. Not looking at an image for face value, but going deeper, like: this person looks comfortable in this image; they must have said something beforehand.

I'm dyslexic—diagnosed late into my academic career—and because of that wasn't a very good student. But I would always try to force myself to write or to write with photography. It terrified me, but I think one of the most beautiful things about photography is that it encourages you to confront your fears in order to produce an image worth the eye's investigation. I can't understand people if I don't understand their story, so I have to do a lot of background reading. Reading and listening to stories helped me practice writing, and that eventually morphed into me adding editorial written words or creative photo captions. Eventually the long hours paid off, and now I can't photograph if I'm not reading and writing about a story or image. Go figure.

I took classes at community college. But straight out of high school, I worked nonstop every single day, trying to look at something different, something beyond what was in the news. I don't necessarily like to call what I cover as "my beat." I like to call it a "core." And my core is *belonging*. It's *home* in the most general sense of it.

Immigration is part of the definition of home, so is labor rights. I'm interested in these topics and read on them, so when I do get those assignments, I'm already prepared. Assignments in these areas can be emotionally difficult, but I've made that decision and understand the consequences. For example I covered a mother's decision whether to return to Mexico at the cost of losing the love and admiration of her daughter or stay in Chicago and continue to struggle financially. That one hit me especially hard because they lived an eight-minute walk from where I was, and she reminded me of my mother. I was talking to and photographing a neighbor, a person that's a part of my community.

I've ways related to some degree to what that general topic is. It provides me room to experience, to grow, to add to the wider conversation, to spread my wings—but at the cost that my wings might burn sometimes if I get too close. I'm struggling with that now, but find the comfort in talking with friends who are in a similar *chamba*.

They warn of bitterness and isolation. But it isn't anything I haven't dealt with before.

In 2019, I knew I was going to be displaced from Pilsen because of rising rents. I was looking for a meaningful story out of town. I went to the local cafe and talked to the elders, and they said, "You should go to Salinas, California. It's a farm- working community, surrounded by agriculture, and they're dealing with something very similar to what we're dealing with here in Pilsen." As I started researching, I got a newsletter from Catchlight, a nonprofit that pairs photographers with local newsrooms across the country. By chance, they were looking for pitches for Salinas. So I pitched them and was accepted as one of four inaugural Catchlight Fellows and moved to Salinas.

There was an affordable housing crisis that needed to be talked about. People who have contributed to this society are unable to pay for their rent or are in housing conditions that they're not safe to be in. I found one of the most important elements to that story in its connection to Pilsen was through labor. Over the years there have been farm workers who would want better pay or better working conditions, so they would go to the Midwest and work in cookie factories, or be machinists, or learn how to weld.

The elders that I had been talking to in Pilsen were a part of that migration from California to Chicago or from Texas to Chicago. We don't realize how interconnected we all are in this country. This idea of alienation or political identities is a product of a wall on the border that is the personification of discrimination against people of color regardless of where they come from.

The intention for the Salinas project was for the team covering the story to be useful and not stand out too much. Being a stranger there was a new feeling for me. So I knew I wanted to do something that included the input of community members. We did community meetings. We surveyed. We informed people about what we were doing along the way. I lived on the east side of Salinas, which is where the majority of my audience lived.

I worked in conjunction with Catchlight and an affiliate newspaper of *USA Today*, so there were reporters and editors involved. The deliverable, the end product, was always to provide something that was thorough. Images are always helpful for stories that are heavily reliant on data or numbers. Photography provides something that can accompany that research so it becomes a complete piece: This is how the housing crisis became what it is. This is what's going on today. Here are some tips and tricks from experts that you can apply today, like establish relationships with your landlords, know your rights, etcetera.

My approach is always evolving. What I'm doing at the moment is applying a scientific method into something as creative as photography with intention. So there's hypothesis, there are questions, there's research, there's surveying, There's all this stuff that inevitably would inform the way that I take pictures—not dictate the way that I take pictures, but inform. There's the emotional aspect, like: "What does it feel like to live near polluted areas or near highways? How are the people stressing out? What does that look like?" That's photography. The data aspect of, say, the health or economic impact of stress, those numbers will allow me to ask questions, referring back to that Capa quote, that will allow me to get closer.

Everybody has a camera in their phone and can become a "citizen journalist." I would encourage anyone to meditate on those choices. Photographing injustices can be very damaging. The video of George Floyd, where a young woman happened to be going to the store one day and took out her phone to document a horrific scene, a murder—that person is traumatized by what she saw. In fact everybody saw it. That's not unique at all.

Seeing hard things all the time does affect you. Take it from somebody who has witnessed secondary pain, or countless murders and death just by living life: be comfortable with the choice you make, try to understand the consequences whatever they might be, and don't burn out. Take care of your own mental health.

I'm right there with you. Still working on it. I sometimes wake up at 2:30 in the morning thinking I'm dreaming, but in reality I'm remembering something. One of the many shootings, a moment of mistreatment, a fact hard to swallow. My heart will be ready to pop out of my chest. That's not sustainable for a very long time. But it is something that I chose when I decided to become a photographer even if I didn't understand it fully.

You have to learn how to take care of those moments. Running helps. It makes the beating of the heart familiar, and you can train your mind and body to calm it in the worst or best of situations.

If you do this work and become bitter, you've essentially lost some part of yourself. Try to prevent that from happening at all cost—for your own sake, but also for the sake of everyone that is in front of the camera or looking at your work. If you do, you've championed a part of yourself and have entered a world beyond what was previously thought was unreachable.

Most importantly, we need to learn how to love people. Love people at their worst and at their best, at their faults and successes. It's one of the most difficult things to do, but without it we cannot seek what we want the most. And by "we" I mean our communities.

FOR MORE INFORMATION:
https://sebastianhidalgo.squarespace.com
https://sebastianhidalgo.squarespace.com/project/salinas
https://www.catchlight.io

'Activism Is Love'

CHOKWE ANTAR LUMUMBA, *38, is the mayor of Jackson, Mississippi.*
EBONY LUMUMBA, *38, is associate professor and chair of the Department of English, Foreign Languages, and Speech Communication at Jackson State University. The Lumumbas met in kindergarten in Jackson and married in 2012. Chokwe Lumumba, a graduate of Tuskegee University and Texas Southern University Law School, was elected in 2017. His late father Chokwe Lumumba (formerly Edwin Finley Taliaferro) served as Jackson's mayor for a year until his death in 2014. Ebony Lumumba, a graduate of Spelman College, earned her PhD in English from the University of Mississippi.*

EBONY: I can go back to being four or five years old and seeing my mother refuse to buy dolls that didn't look like us and instead buying the materials to make ones that did. That moment sticks out so keenly because it's where I came to an understanding that there is an entire movement against who we are fundamentally. It was my introduction into thinking critically about the many ways that we are oppressed as people of color—something as simple as the absence of a baby doll that looks like me to reinforce my identity and rightful space that I hold within society.

CHOKWE: I distinctly remember being five years old at home alone with my older sister when the phone rang. My mother was a flight attendant, so she was often gone during the week. And my father would be off working. So my sister, who's nearly five years older, would look after me. The voice on the phone talked about our father, who was leading anti-Klan rallies and marches, and then told my sister, "I'm gonna kill you and your little brother." It was evident they had eyes on us in the house. I remember going to hide in my parents' closet with a knife until Daddy got home.

I didn't have dreams of bogeymen. I had dreams of the KKK. I had the privilege of growing up with my hero—my father. Out of admiration for what he did, I absolutely knew from my early childhood that I wanted to be engaged in something that was a part of the bigger work of trying to build self-determined communities and trying to improve my community.

EBONY: Activism is a deliberate response to circumstances and challenges. I leave it that broad because in the work that I do as a literature professor, a writer, and an artist, I've seen activism take on so many forms. Just as oppression has so many tentacles and manifestations, activism has to be that diverse and multifaceted as well. It can't only be reactionary. It has to be forward thinking, has to establish a standard before these oppressions and repressive practices take place.

Being an activist necessitates thoughtfulness. It has to be genuine. It has to be organic. It has to be calculated. I use this variety of terminology because I think, of late, we have seen activism be mis-defined. We've seen it go through a sort of pejorative moment where activists are shamed or confused with folks who create chaos. And that's not what activism is.

CHOKWE: In the simplest of terms, I think activism is love. It is an unyielding love that says, "I can't stand for the oppression that I see. I can't stand to see people subjugated. I can't stand to see inequity. I can't stand to see the harm anymore."

Most people think activists are angry or mad. And yes, there is a discontent; it's a refusal to accept the status quo. But I think of something my father said: "If you don't love the people, sooner or later you will betray the people." When you think about fighting for people or putting yourself in harm's way, I don't think that there's a greater expression of love for people than that.

EBONY: I think back to stories that have trickled down through my family. When the neighborhood didn't have full access to a store because of segregation and discrimination, my great-grandmother led the charge to start growing their own food and trading and bartering among themselves. She would buy the entire truck of produce from a white farmer and sell it to her community members and her neighbors at a more fair price. And she was able to build this trove to lend to her neighbors so that they could own their own spaces. That was activism at the grassroots level.

It's something that I've always seen, so it feels natural to respond to a circumstance that is repressive or unjust with action. In raising our girls, we hope that what they're gleaning from being raised around us and our family is that you respond boldly to acts of oppression against yourselves, of course, but also your communities and other communities as well, who could benefit from your support.

CHOKWE: My grandmother worked for the local chapter of SNCC (Student Nonviolent Coordinating Committee) in Detroit. Just recently, going through some documents, I learned how my grandparents were the lead plaintiffs in a lawsuit as their community was succumbing to eminent domain, which took over their homes and their community for a highway system.

I think that was contagious for my father, who out of that intense love to want to see change felt the need to be a revolutionary nationalist freedom fighter. He knew his career as a lawyer—and later as Mayor of Jackson several years before I was elected—had to be a manifestation of that greater work that he was trying to do. Ultimately, I think that it all hinges on the fact that oppression is the greatest organizer of all time.

My father moved from Detroit to Mississippi in the early1970s and had been working with a group called the Republic of New Africa, focused on building self-determined communities. That had culminated in an armed engagement and gunfire with the police. He ultimately returned to Detroit to get his law degree and become a civil rights lawyer.

My parents didn't tell us what to think, they wanted to teach us how to think. They thought that giving us a sense of community, a sense of activism, was as important as giving us food, water, and shelter. They had given their lives to the movement so much so that they believed that they had to give their most precious resource.

We moved from New York to Jackson when I was five. My father had no job waiting. We had no relatives there. We moved to Jackson so that my parents could teach us to be part of the movement. They started the Malcolm X Grassroots Center for self-determination and self-defense where we did political education, summer camps for children, martial arts training and so forth trying to be a resource to the community. I had to learn how to do security outside of the building at age eight!

Before setting up his law practice, my dad had to take the Mississippi Bar Examination. Even that was a struggle. After passing the test, they asked him because of his activist past whether he was going to try to overthrow the state of Mississippi. He paused and said, "Absolutely, but I'm gonna do it in a legal way."

I was ingrained in activism, but at the same time my lived experiences made it personal. I experienced racism in my junior high classroom regularly. Derogatory phrases and comments were commonplace and accepted; rebel flags were displayed; and my classmates cheered when they heard Nat Turner was killed in his rebellion. I spoke out against those things, and I had to wage war with adults for decisions like not standing for the Pledge of Allegiance, which I considered a contradiction to our history. I think the school was surprised when they called my mother in and she supported me.

Another time when a teacher referred to me in a way that he didn't refer to other students, I lashed out and was given an in-school suspension. My father said, "Listen, if you suspend my son for that, then I'm gonna take off my work day and come teach him in school. And then I'm gonna sue you for the time I lost at work." They called his bluff, and he did it—came to school and then filed suit. They took it off my record.

EBONY: As I came of age, I started to understand the necessity to perform these very basic, practical forms of activism in your household and in your own community. We had the headshot of the first black Miss Mississippi on our refrigerator for years to reinforce the value of diverse beauty and our own identities. On the same theme, I remember my father driving two or three hours to find a black doll to give to my sister and me for Christmas one year. He drove that far because at the time it wasn't available anywhere near our city, the state capital of Mississippi.

I also think about the concerted efforts my parents made to ensure that we were reading certain books, that we had seen certain films. It's become canonical now, but we were watching *Roots* when I was seven or eight and not really able to process all the complex themes. But that time was sacred. We were going to watch it as a family, and then we were going to discuss what we saw and what we didn't understand.

It made it clear to me that my parents wanted to be our resource for information about what was right, what was wrong, and what we would encounter as we grew and developed. I remember my mother pushing back against certain standards in the classrooms in my elementary school and these assumptions that were made about black students versus white students. Seeing the consistency in my parents' immediate and bold response whenever oppression reared its head taught us to never shrink back from responding to injustice.

My father was the only black man on bank and real estate boards.

My mother made tremendous sacrifices to become the first black female stockbroker for Dean Witter in Mississippi. She had small children and had to study and be away from us throughout that process, but she made it clear to us why she was doing it. It wasn't for career advancement; she wanted us to understand that if she could do it, then we certainly could and that she should not have had to be the first to do it. This was the early 1990s!

We had a family photo album. But it wasn't conventional. There weren't just images and captions of moments. There were newspaper clippings about family members who had marched for certain things, clippings about family members who had been disenfranchised.

At certain moments—it may have been when we had an issue at school or when we were not responding to something in the way that we should have—my parents would pull out the album and say, "We're going to read this article and discuss this moment. This is your family. And this is what happened to us." We were being taught the many faces of oppression so we could recognize them and so that it would be second nature to respond to it.

And so now, in our professions—with Chokwe as mayor and me in academia—we're keenly aware of the way that these things manifest regardless of environment. The more recent discourse about diversity and equity and inclusion has become dominant, but we're still very clear about how much ground those efforts do not cover.

I've been a voracious reader since I was seven or eight. I think it's impossible to truly read texts from just about any canon and not want to be involved in community, not want to respond to inequities, not want to make an impact. And that's what I found myself wanting to do. I'm not saying that every text illuminates realities and historical truths; they don't. But what I found myself doing at ten or eleven was reading texts and wondering, *Where are my people?*

I loved reading, but never saw myself. That didn't make me want to stop reading. It made me want to find the books where we were. Then, ultimately, in this career that I have now, it made me want to write the books where we will be.

I knew the stories existed in my family because we went over them at the dinner table. When we got home past curfew, we had to sit there and go through the album and read about what had happened to our family members in unjust societies.

I knew the stories existed, but they hadn't been documented. So that is where my activism comes in today—in the way that I accomplish telling those stories in my writing, my teaching, my art. It grew out of noticing the same thing my mother noticed in the dolls, in her stock brokerage, the same thing that my father noticed in his community— that there is an absence, a gap, an inequity. *How do I change that*? And so my career has grown out of that.

My parents did fill one gap. They would assign us books that we weren't reading in school—and then have us write book reports about them. In our household, we had Dr. King's *Letter from Birmingham Jail*, Sojourner Truth's speeches. Alice Walker. Richard Wright.

All this made me even more curious about the texts that weren't focused on our communities. I'm a lover of Shakespeare's tragedies. But I read them now through the lens of looking for the disenfranchised characters, looking for the characters who have blackness projected onto them through their actions. I read Faulkner very differently from some of my colleagues. I'm reading for the identities of the characters of color and the black characters, who are oftentimes more thin than their counterparts in the text.

The last thing I'll say about this is I remember being in graduate school as the only black person in just about all of my classes. And there's a moment in your trajectory as an academic where you're deciding on your specialization. What are you going to write about, research about?

At that point, perhaps surprisingly to everything I've mentioned, I was resisting writing about and focusing on black life and literature because I thought that was going to be expected and that I was going to have to prove myself with these other, more well-accepted genres and canons of literature. But I remember sitting in that class and looking around the table and being the only black person in that class—professor included—and thinking, *If not me, then who? If I don't demonstrate my sincere love for my foundation and my heritage and my community, and do it with this authentic appreciation, who do I expect to do it?*

CHOKWE: One of the themes of both of our stories is that once you're exposed to activism, once you're exposed to knowledge and understanding of what people experience, then it's no longer a choice, right? It becomes a part of your identity from the careers you choose to what makes someone attractive to you.

My wife is not only beautiful, but part of that is being equally yoked and purposeful in the decision of how we would name our children. From a biblical sense, we believe that the power of life and death is in the tongue. We had a part of our history as a people robbed from us—the legacy of meaning in our names and the cultural connection to what African names mean to us and how we choose to name our children. When our ancestors were stolen, their names were also taken. We believe deliberate naming is reclamation in the face of that inhumane injustice. It is reparative and part of our act of self-determination.

My father was born Edwin Finley Taliaferro in Detroit in 1947. He changed his name to Chokwe Lumumba after Dr. King was assassinated. Ebony—whose own name means black—and I have named our daughters Nubia and Alaké. Nubia means beautiful blessing. Alaké means one to be made much of.

For me, growing up in the 1980s in Jackson with the name Chokwe Antar Lumumba was, well let's just say there were never key chains with my name on them! But now, having grown in that space and being educated, there's nothing more beautiful than an African name when I run into it. There's nothing more satisfying than knowing we can name our children African names. Knowing my wife's story, there's nothing more satisfying than when I see our seven-year-old have that same insatiable desire to read and learn and have her picture, her view, of what brilliance and what ability looks like actually look like her.

It's so important that parents and young people be intentional in seeking out information and educating themselves. There are books that I lean on for the truth. Whenever my father would do a black history speech, he'd start off by saying, "You know it's a shame that we're still teaching our children that Christopher Columbus discovered America. America wasn't lost, Columbus was! And long before he and his comrades in Spain figured out that the world wasn't flat, you had Africans traveling to and from the continent of Africa to this continent, this country. They've found totem poles to prove that." He often wasn't invited back!

I wanted to be around him. On the occasions I would go to court with him, I'd see this sea of people who looked like me just pleading guilty to charge after charge and being sentenced to time. And it dawned on me as a little boy, it just seemed like everyone couldn't be guilty. Right? And that evolved into an understanding that not everyone could afford to profess their innocence.

Seeing all the inequity within our justice system, I did not see myself going into elected office. What I was raised on was more antagonistic towards electoral politics and more directed at action. My journey became kind of the evolution of asking what are the best ways to organize and basically coming to the conclusion that if you can only organize people who think like you, you're not much of an organizer.

So as mayor now, while looking at issues like potholes that in the grand scheme of things may seem minor compared to other threats, it is understanding what Amilcar Cabral spoke of when he said that people aren't fighting for the ideas in our heads, they're fighting to win material benefits. Essentially—and I'm paraphrasing—it's the desire to live good, safe lives and to assure a future for their children. So that's the way I see electoral office. I don't see it as the end. I see it as a means to an end, and our end has to be to build self-determined, equitable communities of dignity.

Some degree of compromise is necessary. But what I am unyielding on is that I don't compromise my principles for which I not only lead, but guide my life. These are the principles of self-determination, whether or not people are gaining greater access over their lives, whether people are being enriched in a way that democratizes power.

When I'm asked for advice about how to become more active, I think it returns to love. Your activism doesn't necessarily have to be that you stand up on the table and shout about discrimination or exploitation. It can be the execution of compassion that you show to an individual. It can be the recognition, even in a private setting, to say, "Listen, I want to support you and want you to know that this isn't right. And so we need to find collectively what the solution is."

Any young person that is trying to find their purpose, whether they are a part of an activist community or not, I always give them the words of Frantz Fanon, who wrote *The Wretched Earth*, that, "Each generation must discover its mission and fulfill it or betray it." That's such a profound notion to me: that we're all searching for what our purpose is. We're all searching for what our contribution will be to this world. But once we discover it, we have the responsibility to be bold enough to walk in it.

EBONY: I think if I add anything, it would be to encourage young people to leave whatever space they inhabit better than they found it. I remember being in those classrooms in high school and in middle school and knowing that something wasn't right or hearing something that wasn't right. Even with the support of family, speaking up is scary. Popularity is valuable, and it's difficult to stand out. But one of the motivating things is I knew that I wouldn't be the last black student or black female student or female student in that space. And I had accountability to whomever was coming behind me. And that was a motivating factor: that I could not leave this space without leaving it a little bit better or without making an impact if I have the capability for doing that. The truth is you always have the power to do it.

We can't think about "microwave" activism: that you're going to make a stand and then that change is going to happen quickly. That you are going to get to benefit from it. It's not that fast. So we've got to be content with planting seeds and understand that—and I'm stealing this from an African proverb that Chokwe uses quite a bit—we're sitting under the shade because someone else planted a seed long before us. So we talked about our grandparents and I talked about my great grandparents and the reason that I can sit in this office, the reason that I was able to even attend the schools where I got my graduate degree as a black person was because someone else planted a seed that they did not get to see the fruit of.

I tell my students that it's important to understand that even the small chipping away at the surface of oppression matters and share that my goal for them from interactions that we have is that they foster and maintain intellectual curiosity and question everything. When you're questioning everything, that's going lead you to these sources that my husband has mentioned. That's going to lead you to want to know more about this event or this date or this person, or this text or this quotation. It leads to historical honesty and accuracy when we are intellectually curious. And it doesn't always mean you have to read 500-page history books. That's not everybody's jam.

We've got a three-year-old and a seven-year-old, and the seven-year-old is in that stage of asking profound questions. She wants to understand what she's seeing, what she's absorbing, what's being told to her. She'll say, *My teacher said this. Why is this true?* And that sort of thing. When you have small children, the questions can be overwhelming. But we are determined to answer those questions and to encourage more questions. Sometimes it drives us crazy, but I don't want her to ever feel like there are ever too many questions to ask.

There's always another question to ask about everything. And I think if we adopt this sort of mantra of just being curious, being intellectually curious about everything, about what the media tells us, about what our history books tell us, about what has been accepted as historical fact, then we will get to a much more equitable space.

FOR MORE INFORMATION:
www.jacksonms.gov/departments/office-of-the-mayor/
https://www.mojomama.org/founder/

'Life After Hate'

CHRISTIAN PICCIOLINI, 49, *is a former neo-Nazi extremist turned anti-hate activist. Based in Chicago, he is also an author, speaker, and podcaster.*

ALL I COULD THINK to say was, "I'm sorry, Mr. Holmes." He embraced me, and he forgave me. He encouraged me to forgive myself. He recognized that mine wasn't the story of some broken, going-nowhere kid who was going to just join a gang and go to prison. He knew that this was the story of every young person who was vulnerable, who was searching for identity, community, and purpose, and then hit a wall and was unable to find it and went down a dark path. He made me promise one thing: that I would tell my story to whoever would listen. I've been doing it ever since.

I wasn't born into hate. I had a relatively normal childhood. My parents are Italian immigrants who settled on the south side of Chicago, where they eventually opened a small beauty shop. They struggled to survive, often working seven days a week, fourteen hours a day.

Quality time with my parents was pretty nonexistent. Even though I knew they loved me very much, growing up, I felt abandoned. I started to withdraw, become very angry. One day, when I was fourteen, I was in an alley smoking a joint, and a man with a shaved head and tall black boots came up to me. He snatched the joint from my lips and said, "That's what the communists and the Jews want you to do to keep you docile."

I'd been trading baseball cards and watching *Happy Days*. I didn't really know what a Jew was. But for fourteen years, I'd felt marginalized. I was lost. It was as if this man in this alley had offered me a lifeline.

The man, who was America's first neo-Nazi skinhead, quickly

radicalized me. I started to listen to the rhetoric and believe it. Then, I started to recruit others by making white power music. Within a few years, I became the leader of that infamous organization.

For the next eight years, I saw friends die. I saw others go to prison and inflict untold pain on countless victims and their family's lives. I heard horrific stories from young women in the movement who'd been brutally raped by the very men that they were conditioned to trust. I, myself, committed acts of violence against people solely for the color of their skin, who they loved, or the god they prayed to. I stockpiled weapons for what I thought was an upcoming race war. Twenty-five years ago, I wrote and performed racist music that found its way to the internet decades later and partially inspired a young white nationalist to walk into a sacred Charleston, South Carolina, church and sense-lessly massacre nine innocent people.

Then my life changed. At nineteen, I fell in love with a girl who was not in the movement, who didn't have a racist bone in her body. We got married and had our first son. When I held him in my arms, I began asking myself: *Who am I? A neo-Nazi hate monger or a caring father and husband?*

I compromised. I took myself off the streets for the benefit of my family because I was nervous that maybe I could go to jail or end up dead. I stepped back as a leader and instead I opened a record store and sold white power music.

My wife and children left me because I hadn't left the movement and disengaged quickly enough. A friend concerned about my well-being suggested I apply for a job where she worked, at IBM. I thought she was crazy. I was a closeted ex-Nazi, covered in hate tattoos. I didn't even own a computer. But I got the job.

Then I became terrified to learn that they'd be putting me back at my old high school to install their computers. This was a high school where I had been expelled twice, committed acts of violence against students, against faculty, and had gotten into fights with a black security guard—Mr. Holmes.

When I got to the school, Mr. Holmes didn't recognize me. I didn't know what to do. I followed him to the parking lot. That's when I apologized, and he told me to tell my story.

From 2000 to 2004, I did tell my story in some circles, but mainly I worked on myself. I held myself accountable, but I wouldn't have considered myself an activist at that point. Then on July 3, 2004, at age thirty-one, I had my moment. My brother was killed by an African American gang member. My first thought was not hate or revenge. Instead I realized there were a lot of people of all kinds who didn't have anyone to turn to. I wasn't doing enough to help other people who needed my help.

That's when I started doing the work that I'm doing now. I started to be more vocal about my story. I wasn't just keeping it to smaller circles anymore. I was now starting to tell the world that, number one, we have a problem that's brewing. And, number two, there's something we can do about it if we act now, and I'm doing it and it's working, so pay attention. People started to pay attention, and I think that that's what ended up formalizing it.

It started as this support network called Life after Hate that I co-founded with a friend, because what I recognized was not only that I had nobody else to talk to for help, neither did they. Even though they had left the movement years prior, they'd never really talked about their involvement with their significant others or their loved ones.

While I was doing that work with those who were no longer in the movement, people started coming to me and saying, "Hey, I'm *in* the movement. I need help." Taking the first step and asking for help disengaging from that movement is also a really strong step forward.

I try to make people more resilient, more self-confident, more able to have skills to compete in the marketplace so that they don't have to blame the *other*. The *other* that they've never met.

All the people I've worked with will tell you the same thing. One, they became extremists because they wanted to belong, not because of ideology or dogma. Two, what brought them out of that extremism was receiving compassion from the people they least deserved it from, when they least deserved it. I challenge everyone to go out and find someone undeserving of your compassion and give it to them. Because I guarantee you, they are the ones who need it the most.

I think activism is being personally invested in the assistance of others who might be marginalized. I think it is just making that decision to be accountable if you're complicit, to give of your privilege if you have it, if you enjoy it, and to make your voice heard, potentially at a risk to you being unpopular because of it. It's putting yourself out there in service.

People who stand up are incredibly brave. After the Parkland shooting, you had the students that banded together and went around the world and made their voices heard and, for a while, were the only responsible people speaking about the issue in a way that people heard it. It's our failure as adults for not making the world a place where they can speak freely and safely about what they might be feeling.

It's really hard for anyone to speak up about wrongs they see injustices. It's especially hard for young people, right? Young people are so consumed with not standing out, trying to fit in, not being outside of the box. Certainly, there are exceptions to that. There are some people who are very independent and not afraid to show that. But I think most young people are averse to being different.

How do you advise somebody to get beyond that discomfort and when they witness something to act on it? Maybe as adults we are not having those conversations with young people we need to have, exposing our own vulnerability with them to let them know that it's okay to expose their own vulnerability with us. Otherwise, we may never have those conversations, and they'll go through life thinking they need to be perfect for us and we need to act perfect for them.

I've written two books, *White American Youth: My Descent into America's Most Violent Hate Movement—and How I Got Out*, and

Breaking Hate: Confronting the New Culture of Extremism. I also have the F*** Your Racist History podcast which explores events that don't make it into the history books, but should. I speak to groups around the world and until recently led an effort called the Free Radicals Project.

I've realized that while *deradicalization* is really important, there's no amount of it that is going to get us out of this mess, because radicalization occurs too fast. So I've shifted my focus to *prevention*. I think the only way we win this is if we prevent future generations from going down this path of hate and extremism. It's not enough to—and I hate to use this analogy—be like a garbage man and come in when the mess has already been made and help clean it up.

Eventually, we have to get to the point where no more messes are being made. So unless I focus on prevention, I just don't see there being much of an impact in the disengagement work that I do. I call it shutting off the "bigot spigot." We have to fix systemic and institutional racism, too. Otherwise, we will always have an environment where there will be an endless line of people for me to help disengage. So my goal is to try and stem the flow from the bigot spigot as much as possible.

FOR MORE INFORMATION:

www.christianpicciolini.com

White American Youth: My Descent into America's Most Violent Hate Movement—and How I Got Out, 2018

Breaking Hate: Confronting the New Culture of Extremism, 2020

'Within the Framework of Politics'

EDWIDGE DANTICAT, 53 is the award winning author of several books— novels, memoir, and collections—for adults, young adults and children. Her memoir, Brother, I'm Dying, won the 2008 National Book Critics Circle Award. The following year she was named a MacArthur Fellow. She was born in Port-au-Prince, Haiti. When she was two, her father came to the United States, where he eventually became a gypsy cab driver. Her mother followed two years later. They remained in the U.S. undocumented for eight years, while Danticat and her brother were raised by an aunt and uncle. After their parents received their papers in 1981, Danticat, then twelve, and her brother joined them in Brooklyn. Her work revolves around themes of social justice, and she has spoken before Congress and at other venues on the need for immigration reform. She now resides with her husband and two teenage daughters in Miami.

FOR ME, I THINK it was when Yusuf Hawkins was brutally killed in 1989. He was a young black man who had gone to a white neighborhood in Bensonhurst to buy a car. This group of young Italian American men were waiting to ambush a group of black young men they thought were coming to a party at the home of one of their ex-girlfriends. They chased Yusuf Hawkins down, beat him, and shot him. I remember going to a march with my brothers right after the murder. There were thousands and thousands of people protesting and demanding justice for Yusuf. This march struck me very much because it reminded me of the power of collectivity—what a bunch of people, putting their voices and bodies together can do. I think, too, it struck me so hard because it's not something that my family would've been able to do in Haiti during the dictatorship.

I define activism as just trying to contribute towards making a better world. My impulse to become involved springs from the way I grew up—in Haiti during a dictatorship. There were members of my family who had left Haiti because of their activism. There were writers and others who bravely spoke out and were disappeared. And when others who had left the country spoke out, they risked having family members still in Haiti massacred. Growing up I was told about these activists who were trying to make a difference by putting their lives on the line. They became flesh and blood to me.

When I came to New York, my parents were very afraid of being too political. But there were moments where they felt they had to act. I remember we marched in 1983 when the FDA announced that Haitians couldn't give blood because they were at high risk for AIDS. Haitians were the only ones singled out by nationality for being at high risk for HIV transmission. The others were hemophiliacs, homosexuals, and heroin addicts. That same year I visited an immigration detention center with our church where my father was a deacon. So I was extremely aware of immigration issues and anti-Haitian biases and other political issues by the time I was fourteen. I also had a chance to observe the lifelong activism of people who are always stepping forward as well as that reluctant type of activism of people like my parents who don't really step forward until they feel, *enough is enough.* My takeaway from it was that one shouldn't be complacent; If there's something you can do, you should try to do it. And so when Abner Louima—who happened to be a member of our church—was beaten and sexually assaulted in Brooklyn by the NYPD a few years after Yusuf was murdered, we marched again.

Even before her first novel, Breath, Eyes, Memory, *was published to acclaim in 1994, Danticat had used her writing to shine a light*

> *on and create a dialogue around social injustices and to serve as a*
> *catalyst for change. She feels more comfortable being described as an*
> *"artivist" than activist, and says she was greatly influenced by the*
> *literature of Haitian writers. Not fluent in English when she arrived*
> *in the U.S., she devoured works written in French in the Haitian*
> *Literature section of her local public library. She says that when she*
> *read those books, she felt like she was back in Haiti. "I started read-*
> *ing to go home really—as a kind of a way of visiting Haiti."*

From the beginning, I wanted my work to have a greater purpose than entertainment. I remember reading an interview with the African American writer Toni Cade Bombara, where she said that writing was her way of participating in the struggle. I wanted my readers to be engaged like that. I wanted them to learn. I wanted them to perhaps act. It would've been hard for me to just write a story for the sake of writing a story. I think part of it is because of my background, but also because I had always read literature that in some ways serves some other purpose. Art for art's sake was not going to be a choice for me.

Of course, there's always a balancing act between art and just preaching. A few years ago, I saw Toni Morrison in conversation with Angela Davis at the New York Public Library. At that talk, Ms. Morrison said that art can be both beautiful and political at the same time. It depends on how you do it. Even the choice not to be political is also political.

For me, the important thing is to tell an engaging story within the framework of politics. There's so much political theater in politics, for example. Even politicians are obsessed with narrative. They're constantly telling us stories, like they're fiction writers.

Storytelling plays an extraordinary role in activism. There's a Haitian proverb that says that if you see old bones on the street, just remember it once had flesh on it. Storytelling puts flesh on bones; it brings people and events back to life.

In 2004 my Uncle Joseph fled to the U.S. after United Nations Peacekeepers killed his neighbors from the roof of his church and his neighbors turned against him. He was eighty-one. He had a valid visa and passport, but when he arrived in the U.S., he requested asylum, and the Department of Homeland Security arrested him and held him in an immigration detention center in Miami. He quickly fell ill there and died in the prison ward shackled to a bed a few days later. We later learned he had been denied his medicine for his high blood pressure and inflamed prostate.

My uncle was reduced to a number. He had an alien number. Every time he was referred to, he was referred to by his number. So in my family memoir, *Brother, I'm Dying*, I really wanted to *(re) flesh* my uncle, put flesh back on his bones, remind people that he was a human being—he was a father, a grandfather, a preacher, an uncle. Storytelling is a powerful way to do that, and in addition to the book, I told his story to a Congressional subcommittee and on *60 Minutes* to actually try and change policy.

Sometimes we read a novel and it's like we know the people in the book better than we know people in our own lives. So storytelling is a powerful tool of advocacy. You can recite some statistics to try and advocate. We're living in a moment now where someone will say that nine hundred thousand people have died of COVID, and you think, *Wow, that's a lot of people.* But It can be even more powerful if you tell the story of just one family who lost someone who is very crucial to them or integral to their community. The story makes that person more than a vague number.

I've had two experiences now with storytelling as a sort of engagement of the world. A friend of mine who was a dean at a Florida law school here in Miami invited me to talk to a group of immigration lawyers in training. She explained that they might have hearings for as many as twenty clients in one day. And each hearing to determine whether the person got to stay in the U.S. might last only five minutes.

Five minutes to make that person's case to the judge and determine their future. And sometimes that person is a child, an unaccompanied minor who doesn't even understand what's going on.

So the lawyers read my story collection, *Krik? Krak!* It's the title of the book, but it's also a call and response storytelling technique in Haiti. If you want to tell a story, you say, *krik*. And the response of the listeners who want to hear your story is, krak. The lawyers and I talked about how there were stories in the book about people who could be like their clients—people who were undocumented in different ways.

We talked about how to create a narrative around that person's experiences, which were something harrowing. Mass migration is driven by group circumstances. So people have similar stories. But what's the singularity of that one person's—your client's—story?

You are appearing before a very hostile audience. Try to have a beginning, middle, and end to the story, have an arc: What the person was before, what they're doing now. Find some very interesting details about the person, just as we would do with a character; again, stress their singularity. And then try to be as vivid as possible, try to infuse all five senses into your narrative. These are things that I use when I write to make that person stand out and their story stand out.

Besides these lawyers, I often talk to a group of medical interns about how to *listen* to the stories that people are telling. How to read between the lines and figure out what they're telling you and what they're not telling you. What they're afraid to tell you. I talked to a group doing internships in psychiatry after they read *Breath, Eyes, Memory*. We discussed how to examine people who have been tortured, who have been raped while trying to get here. So I do think literature can be used in a functional way in the world.

I know that a lot of people look at all the problems we face and ask: "What can I do? What difference can I make?" I keep going back to Toni Morrison. During the height of the civil rights movement, she had her small children at home, and she was an editor at Random House.

She said she had to start where she was. So what she did was she edited the activists. She edited Angela Davis's autobiography. She also edited Muhammad Ali's autobiography. She broadened their platforms.

So start where you are. You are not powerless. Spend your money wisely, with people who won't use it to oppress others. Reduce your climate footprint as much as you can. Volunteer. Vote. The small things we do add up to large things collectively. We started this conversation about the power of numbers, *collectivity*. Sometimes just acting and showing up together can make a big difference.

FOR MORE INFORMATION:
www.edwidgedanticat.com
edwidgedanticat/facebook.com

'Calling Out Discrimination'

BRIAN JON, *20, is the founder of the New Jersey–based Asian American Youth Council (AAYC). He is from Tenafly, New Jersey, and attends Lehigh University He has chronicled his life in the autobiography,* I am The Brian.

I WAS A HIGH school freshman when I heard about a teacher's hateful racial slur. That was unacceptable to me, particularly as a Korean American. At first I wrote a very sincere letter to the principal, asking him to take action against the teacher. I didn't think I would get a response. And I was right. That made me realize that unless the entire student body or a large number of students were interested in the situation, the teachers and the administration were not going to care. I thought about this in a bigger context. In the U.S, politicians may change a law or write a bill, but it's usually based on pressure from the majority. So I figured the best way for me to try to get the school board of education's attention was to gather as many signatures as possible.

I came to New Jersey from South Korea at the age of six with my single mother. I did not know any English, except for, "Hello." I was able to blend in pretty quickly. I learned the language and became involved in numerous activities. By high school, I had won various awards for my art, sung at Lincoln Center, made first trombone in our school band, emceed New Jersey's annual K-pop contest, and swam in the Junior Olympics.

I also was a cheerleader! As one of the biggest kids in my class, I was an uncommon sight amongst the bubbly—and slim—cheerleaders. Before joining the cheerleading team, I was a promising wrestler and played football. That changed when my best friend Ethan blurted out over the phone a chilling confession: "Sometimes, I don't have the will to live anymore."

Ethan badly wanted to join the cheerleading team. But he was petrified because he thought people would make assumptions about his sexuality and pressure him to admit what he wasn't prepared to; he needed more time to face the harsh prejudice in our school against his sexual orientation. Worse yet, his conservative Asian parents might get a whiff of this "rumor."

Seeing Ethan suffering made me think of the many different kinds of social stigma that people face—be it sexual orientation, ethnicity, or disability. If Dr. King stood up for the millions against the entire nation, I could stand up for one person against my school. The next day, I went to the cheerleading coach to talk to her about a tryout so Ethan wouldn't feel alone.

Ethan also became a cheerleader. I think I helped provide him with the confidence to believe that he should always be able to pursue whatever he wants. Especially, when he was good at what he wanted. There's no reason for others to judge because you're doing what you love.

Activism is an idea followed by the act that is motivated by good intent and the desire to maximize happiness. It tries to fix the wrongs in the world by bringing justice—not always through legislation, but socially. To me, activists are people who do their best in performing these acts with a goal of making the world a better place.

I learned not to be afraid of what others think from two prominent figures in my life: my mother and my cousin, Yunji. Raising a child while working was not easy for my single mother, but she worked just as hard to help me pursue my interests and encourage independence. She'd hear me out whenever I wanted to do something and even if she was worried for my well-being, would eventually be supportive. Her support provided improvements in shaping AAYC and has helped me become the activist I am today.

My cousin Yunji has always been an inspiration. She was born with cerebral palsy. Our parents were working, so I would spend most of my childhood with her. At times I wouldn't even notice that she was disabled because she was always sharing her dreams and passions with me. One of the main reasons I was able to voice my opinions and speak up for myself was by watching Yunji. She has a very clear idea of what she needs to express and what she believes in.

I was fortunate to get into Bergen County Technical High School, a magnet school that's ranked as one of the best high schools in New Jersey. In 2017, on the first day of school of my freshman year, a Spanish teacher was said to have made discriminatory comments to Korean students, telling them, "I hate Koreans." The teacher apparently made this comment six times in two different classes.

The students who were present, including Koreans, did not seem taken aback by the comments, nor did they photograph or record the incident like other minority students who have experienced discrimination by teachers. Black and Hispanics who have experienced discrimination by teachers have often called it out, but I think the majority of Koreans, especially immigrants, are under this preconceived notion that we should be quiet and respect our elders (which requires us to not speak back). At the same time, there were also seniors that didn't want complications, nor a new teacher, that would end up causing disruptions during their college application process.

In order to keep its prestigious reputation, the school intended to quietly close the case. Although I wasn't in either of the Spanish classes, I was taken aback by the comments. I started a petition. This led to gathering more than 1600 signatures, which I later brought to a Board of Education meeting. With my effort, the Spanish teacher was not able to teach anymore. Also importantly, this incident led youth councils all over New Jersey to gather to raise the voices of Korean Americans.

About three months after the incident, I established the Korean American Youth Council (KAYC) to address discrimination, share our cultural values, and become a "bridge" between the U.S. mainstream and the Korean community. After working on behalf of KAYC for some time with mayors, senators, and representatives, I realized that I could have an even larger positive impact by establishing a council that embraced all Asian Americans rather than a single ethnicity. So I founded AAYC. The Council addresses various current issues regarding race, gender, politics, and society which are impacting the well-being and status of our community. Most importantly, we focus on raising social awareness about political rights, which most of our previous Asian American generations have not been able to enjoy within our society.

We've canvassed for and endorsed political candidates, successfully lobbied for legislation that would make the history of Asian Americans mandatory in New Jersey's curriculum, and spoken out about the wave of hate crimes against Asian Americans that have occurred in Atlanta, New York, and various other places throughout these past years. Throughout these experiences, we have built relationships with New Jersey political figures including Governor Phil Murphy, Senator Cory Booker, Congressman Andy Kim, and many local politicians.

Outside the political arena, one of our biggest recent achievements came in working with Governor Murphy to proclaim October 21, 2021, as New Jersey's first Korean Hanbok Day. Hanbok literally means "Korean clothing." Our celebration featured a fashion show, traditional Korean music, and a traditional wedding. It's an example of how we want to normalize the idea of the cultural diversity in our country. Tammy Murphy, New Jersey's first lady, was the keynote speaker.

There are several requirements of applicants for AAYC, including showing your report card, writing an essay, and getting a recommendation letter. At first I chose the members, but now we have an Admission Committee made up of local college professors and others.

One thing I realized after talking with my mother was that in order for an organization to be effective during teenage years, parents should be on the same page and ready to be involved. Our members have to be students with like-minded parents that want to be fully supportive of their dreams. So the Council currently interviews parents, not only students, to see how knowledgeable they are about society and the mindset they have to contribute to our society.

The Council's stated mission is to cultivate future Asian American leaders in youth participation through various civic and educational projects. Across the globe, we currently have more than eighty youth activists. Because we believe community service is a lifetime commitment, a lot of the students that entered colleges before I did have continued to spread the word about AAYC. We're trying to create a more responsible Asian American community, throughout which we can continue to develop new norms and practices that enrich not only our own, but the wider American society. That's why we have affiliated youth activists today that are not just from New Jersey or New York, but also from New Zealand, South Korea, Virginia, and California. Our goal is to spread globally.

We're trying to create connections in society that would help us not only participate more in the political fields where we're raising our voices. To help with everything, we have a great group of advisors, including politicians, who have some type of influence in our society.

I want to study business and pursue a career in the finance field. Although I don't want to be a politician, I would still like to challenge myself in an election, at least once in my life. If I do end up running, I would like to run for a position to challenge the title "youngest Korean candidate," aiming for a position that can't realistically be elected at my age, to further open doors for our younger generation that have the courage to take on the challenge. I dream of achieving financial freedom so that I can provide for our second and third generations who have the dream of becoming politicians. I want to be a role model for the Asian community.

FOR MORE INFORMATION:
https://www.asianamericanyouthcouncil.org/
I am The Brian. Saenggak Nanum, 2020.

'Power in Spaces and Places'

BRYAN LEE JR., *39, is founder/director of Colloqate Design, a New Orleans–based nonprofit architecture + urban design practice. He has twelve years experience as an architect, design justice advocate, and organizer with a focus on spatial justice in the built environment. He is the founding organizer of the Design Justice Platform and organized the Design as Protest: National Day of Action.*

WHEN I WAS ELEVEN, my mother was in the Air Force, and we lived in Sicily. Walking through the streets and plazas, I fell in love with this place—sometimes with the people, other times with the architecture. But when I was twelve, things changed. My mother got stationed in New Jersey, and we ended up moving in with my grandmother in Trenton—in a beautiful little row house in a hood.

There was something in the middle of the house that I was afraid of—a staircase that I called "the abyss." The staircase was daunting—cold and dark. Every time my grandmother walked up and down the stairs, her legs would hurt. I remember thinking to myself, *My grandmother shouldn't live in a place where the architecture hurts her body.* Seeing the dissonance between place and space in Sicily and in Trenton, I started to understand what disadvantage and disparity looked like. I decided to become an architect in that moment.

I talk about activism as a necessity, not only to recognize injustice or inequity, but a compulsion to speak out against it. I grew up in a family with a pretty substantial black library—almost entirely nonfiction. Having a deep historical context always makes you aware of the conditions of place. As I got into high school and certainly as I got into college, those readings became very present for me, explaining the ways in which systems were applied, not just to me, but to communities that I was a part of.

I was a military brat, so I jumped back and forth between a lot of places. As a result, in a lot of ways, I was an observer. James Baldwin talked about the difference between him and Malcolm X and Martin Luther King, as being a narrator, an observer. To be active felt like you actually had to be in a place. And the first time that I felt like I was in a place long enough to understand it well enough to be a representative through any activism was in college. That began in response to the Gore and Bush election. And then again, the Kerry and Bush election. Those were the kind of generative moments for me—between 2000 and 2005, from age seventeen to twenty-two.

As a kid, I didn't really know what architecture meant. So my family kind of egged me along. I got my Masters in Architecture in 2008 and after a few years decided to focus on design justice advocacy. Design justice recognizes that race and culture and architecture are inherently connected. It also acknowledges that we want to dismantle the privilege and power structures that actively use architecture to create systems of injustice within the built environment.

Architecture has a role to play in creating racial and cultural equity in space. This isn't new. Back in 1968, Whitney Young, who was the Executive Director of the National Urban League, said our profession's contribution towards the cause of civil rights was, "thunderous silence and complete irrelevance." And he was right. We have perfected a process of design that creates fantastic environments for those with means and wealth, but have turned a neglectful eye towards those without it. As architects we want equality for all, but the problem with that is that our silence when it comes to the issue of injustice in the built environment is complicity. Architecture is a documentarian of inequality and injustice, and the language we use to talk about place and space reveals our values and tells our biases.

Ken Kerr, an architect based in the UK, tells a story that sums up this idea. He notes that the first American house built in wartime Java completely bewildered the natives there. Instead of building walls out of local bamboo, which is closely spaced together to keep out the rain and let in the light and air, the Americans cut holes in the walls to create windows, to let in the light and air.

You see when oppression and injustice are institutionalized and then manifested in our architecture, people have to change their patterns. They change their rhythms. It effectively changes cultural meaning and the relation with space. Architecture has the power to speak the language of the people we serve. We just have to be willing to speak to the people without power—because in the end, language is important, and architecture is a language. And like all languages, it allows us to tell a story, because stories are important, and buildings tell our stories.

Diverse stories are the result of diverse cultures, because culture is important. For people of color in America, there is power in the places and spaces where our culture is recognized, where our stories are told, where our language is valued. Because that is not only good design. That is justice.

For me, it was always about how I would be able to use my skills to occupy space in the name of the communities that have been marginalized and disenfranchised. How do you use these tools not just to claim a spot at a white supremacist table, but to really shutter those systems of oppression and create new worlds that are enveloped in the frameworks of justice that we as movement workers have tried to define over the last one hundred fifty years post Reconstruction?

In 2011, we—the New Orleans chapter of the National Organization of Minority Architects—created a program called Project Pipeline to introduce young people of color to the field of design—creating internships and a path to employment. But in 2014, we changed the program to be focused on social justice, through the built environment. In doing so, we had to create frameworks that were digestible for young people and would year after year radicalize them towards designing spaces that would help them recognize that they have the power to operate and change spaces. We created the term "design justice." Project Pipeline has involved more than fifteen thousand of these young people.

In late November 2016, after Donald Trump had been elected president, a few of us created "Design as Protest: National Day of Action." We organized six hundred people from across the country to meet in workshops to discuss the implications of the election on social justice in the built environment.

Then in 2017, I created my current workplace, a not-for-profit called Colloqate Design. Colloquial + Locate + Collocate: Colloqate. We're a multidisciplinary Architecture + Design Justice practice focused on expanding community access to and building power through the design of social, civic, and cultural spaces.

That same year, after the removal of four Jim Crow monuments revealed deep-seated divisions in New Orleans, we collaborated on a project to imagine new monuments. "Paper Monuments" was, as we described it, "a public art and public history project designed to elevate the voices of the people of New Orleans, as a critical process towards creating new narratives and symbols of our city. . . to honor the erased histories of the people, events, movements, and places that have made up the past three hundred years as we look to the future."

In the years that have followed, we have designed, among other things, a workforce training center in a racially diverse neighborhood in Portland. Oregon, and a K-12 school in Brooklyn. Like all of our projects, these have been virtually completely driven by the community. We've also collaborated on a number of social justice initiatives. One example is "Blights Out," a collective of activists, artists, and architects whose mission is to challenge inequitable development and drive land use policy in New Orleans.

For nearly every injustice in this world, there is an architecture, a design, a plan that was built to sustain it. Knowing that, how do we envision spaces of racial reparation and healing through the design of space? Values are validated through the spaces and places that we design. So the things that we believe in get vested into the built environment. If we believe that we should jail more people, we create more courthouses. Then we put more people in jail. If we believe that certain people should have education, we build more schools.

My advice to those interested in entering the social justice space is first find other people that are engaging in this set of conversations. Nothing we do in this world, we do alone—even if it feels like that. Oftentimes we are given the idea that a lionized individual is the only pathway for success, but all of this work requires collective.

The second thing is to make room for joy, even in challenging harmful systems. I have a dear friend who once told me that we don't organize and march in the streets and be activists so that we can continue to be mad all of time. We do it because at some point we want to be happy. We want to be joyful. So find joy,

I often say that failure is just a rung on the ladder of success. Don't invest all your time in considerations about failure. Find and be around people who are critical, not cynical. That's a fine line, a hard distinction. But critical people start with an openness; cynical people often start with the "no. "

Another suggestion: Write. Oftentimes people neglect how important it is to write things down and to be able to reflect on them many years later. From an early age I started journaling about the type of work I wanted to be doing and about the relationships that I saw as important.

Every year I look back at those words. What I wrote wasn't particularly revelatory, but it gave me the words to eventually search for books that I didn't know I needed, to find the other information I needed.

Finally: Define your values, learn about your values, don't have superficial values. Understand what they are, and understand why you believe that. Take the time to understand yourself.

Care is a very important value. It means that we have to be a part of a beloved community. And if we work for beloved community, then that means that we have to be in community, right? It means that we have to go out and be a part of events and meet with people in a way that is not transactional. Because then when those moments come where your skill set is needed, those people will be able to call on you.

FOR MORE INFORMATION:
Colloqate.org

'To Start a Movement'

PRANJAL JAIN, *21, is an Indian-American organizer and writer from the metropolitan New York City area, who has created numerous social justice events, curricula, and workshops. A member of Cornell University's Class of 2023, she is the founder of Global Girl Network, a primarily GenZ women-led community that inspires storytelling and fosters intercultural dialogue.*

IN MY EIGHTH GRADE social studies class, we were sharing what we wanted to be when were older, and I said, "President." But my teacher said, "You can't be president. You weren't born here." I guess I'd known that, but it didn't really feel like an impediment to me until hearing someone in a position of power tell me that my dreams weren't possible. It felt like a really big betrayal, especially because growing up in this country, I'd always heard that I could be whatever I wanted to be. It made me really upset.

And so that year I wrote to then President Obama asking him why I couldn't be president just because I wasn't born here. I said, "I came to this country when I was six months old. I feel just as American as the kid next to me in class."

To make sure that he got my message, I sent him one hundred letters. He responded, thanking me for my commitment to public service. That made me realize the power of my voice, that my voice is definitely my superpower. And since then I've really valued it and used it to make change.

I had my first real experience with change-making a year or so before writing that letter. When I was ten, I was cyber-bullied by classmates. I told my teachers and my principal, but they really didn't know how to help me, what to tell the girls who were the bullies. A year later, after

I had sort of recovered and come to understand my own power and my own resources, I created a curriculum to fill in that gap that my experience had clearly pointed out.

With the help of my Girl Scouts troop leader, I was able to understand what it means and looks like to create a message, to organize around it, and to start a movement. We focused on equipping young people with the knowledge necessary to share with peers. We also gave administrators tools that emphasize the consequences for bullies rather than focusing on victims. To create the curriculum that complemented those resources, I worked with the Nassau County [NY] District Attorney Kathleen Rice [later a congresswoman] to create something I could take into seventh and eighth grade health classes and teach.

A few years later I discovered that I had been formally undocumented until I was seven. I got my passport at that age, but didn't become naturalized until I was fourteen or fifteen. I was so confused. I remember going to the ceremony, taking the oath, and coming home and being like, "Why did I have to do that?" I ended up missing an important class and test. It was right before Trump got elected and so many different things sort of just clicked. It helped me start understanding my own immigrant identity, especially because I think it doesn't look like most narratives do.

The experience affirmed my commitment to service to the communities I belonged to—young women and undocumented immigrants. It was a call to action for me. So after Trump got elected, I organized a peaceful rally centered around acceptance because I felt our community needed it. Later I organized a vigil for the victims of the Parkland shooting. And the next year, I created a curriculum around menstrual equity and anti-sexual harassment. Then in my senior year of high school, I helped found Gen Z Girl Gang, an organization that is redefining sisterhood for our age.

I think these efforts at change-making—I'm too young to feel comfortable being labeled an "activist"—were born from my own experiences. Honestly, they came from a place of urgency about the state of the world and especially America. With the physical and intuitive characteristics that you'd attribute to me being a young South Asian woman of color, I realized that if I wanted to live and exist authentically, I needed to create that space for myself, and I needed to create that space for others.

This all helped prepare me for what happened next. The summer before my freshman year of college at Cornell, I went back to my birth city, Jaipur, India. Sort of out of curiosity, maybe intuition, maybe just a desire to learn more, I spent my time there speaking to the women of Jaipur, understanding where I came from, who I am a direct byproduct of.

In doing that, I learned their stories and I learned about the power that exists within them. It was really eye-opening, because growing up I always felt like there was no one that really had the same values as I did or looked like me and was doing the kind of work that I wanted to do.

All the women I knew were either the teachers at school or my mom's friends who were all housewives. Not to say that those aren't really important professions and ways of living, but that's not really what I wish for myself. So I just always believed that Indian women and, I guess, a larger majority of women of color, especially when it comes to women from the East, just weren't powerful.

But when I was in India and when I talked to the women from the land that I was born in, I learned that they were all powerful in their own right. It helped me decolonize narratives around power and around productivity and success. It also made me understand more of who I was, where I came from and what transpired for me to be who I am.

I realized that I gained all of that insight through stories, through interviews, through listening and through writing. Then I realized that I could also sort of gift-wrap that entire experience and give it to other girls to do the same. So I did, and that's how Global Girlhood was born. We really center storytelling, intercultural dialogue, and making sure that all these women, with our crazy intergenerational diversity and geographical diversity, find ways to connect with each other and to create long-lasting friendships.

Global Girlhood as an organization wasn't born overnight. When I came back from India with all the stories I'd captured, I just wanted to share them informally on a personal platform. So I started an Instagram account.

Then it became like, "Hey guys, I went to India and I realized this. Oh my God, you guys should try this, too. It's so cool."

From there it became, "Oh, wait, why don't we just bring it to everybody?" I literally just started off with proof of concept. I just acted on what it is that I believed in.

Telling my friends about this was an important part of the process. I think when you are trying to activate and create a movement, you definitely need to start with your friends because those are the ones that are going to believe in you. Those are the ones that are going to help you. They will be the ones that will help you gain and create a lot of traction.

Another piece of advice is to just do. If you don't just try stuff out, you'll never know what works and what doesn't. So it's almost a 100 percent guarantee that you are going to fail.

You are not going to be able to figure out the right model that works right away. But the more you do it, the closer you are to accomplishing whatever you want and serving your community. I think what stops a lot of people is the belief that they don't have what it takes or they don't have the network. But once you start, things will sort of just fall into place or you'll navigate and figure out what works best for you and what doesn't.

Here's a brief portion from one of the many stories we've told on the globalgirlhood.org platform. It's from an interview Saba Mir conducted with Brianna Chandler, a black liberation climate justice, queer justice, and gender justice activist, who is a student at Washington University of St. Louis:

I did go to an all-girls school in high school, and it was a predominantly white, Catholic institution. It's not necessarily something that we could afford, but there was a lot of financial aid given, so not only was there a race divide, there was more of a class divide. Just being there and kind of seeing how I had to change my tone and kind of conform myself to make my white peers more comfortable with me, and just seeing how sometimes white women can understand gender and justice but not necessarily understand racial justice. And just kind of how white women have not always been the best allies to black women.

.I understand that speaking out against injustice and starting projects is easier said than done. So my advice is to look around you for help. When I was organizing against cyber-bullying, I didn't feel like anybody in my school was doing that already or could help me, so I looked out into my larger community and found that my Girl Scouts troop leader was ready to do whatever it took to help me.

So even when you feel helpless and when you feel like you don't know what to do, if you just talk about it, if you just put it out there, and if you're just really sharing with people, something and someone will fall your way and you'll be able to make that a reality. One of the biggest pieces of advice that I give everybody is to just ask for what you want, ask for it all over, ask everybody. And if what you want isn't available, you'll be able to create it with the help of someone else.

I'm sometimes asked what to do if your parents are worried about what might happen if you speak out or act. I'm still navigating this myself, but I will say that, from the age of seventeen onwards, my parents haven't really known what I do in this space and what I do professionally. But they've never discouraged me. They've always been happy when I share certain things to see what I'm up to and where I'm going.

I think you might find this is similar across a lot of young people of color. I think the idea of change-making looks very different in the East and has a lot more different connotations and dangers associated with it than it does in the West. Also, just in general there is a generational gap. It's hard to explain what you do to your parents if they haven't grown up here and if they aren't really in the loop with what's going on.

I'm majoring in Industrial and Labor Relations at Cornell. I've never been one to tie myself to a specific career path. I have too many interests for that. Eventually, I want to do journalism. I would love to go to law school. I'd love to continue supporting young women into office, by being part of their campaign and serving as a campaign manager or in another position like that. I'd love to continue building out Global Girlhood. I'd love to be involved with other nonprofits. That's a lot of different things—but hopefully all with the intention of empowering young women in whatever capacity that may look like.

FOR MORE INFORMATION:
Instagram and Twitter: @pranjalljain
pranjal-jain.com
globalgirlhood.org

'We Are Still Suing'

JACQUELINE DE LEÓN, *is a staff attorney specializing in voting rights at the Boulder, Colorado-based Native American Rights Fund (NARF), the oldest, largest nonprofit legal organization defending the rights of Native American tribes, organizations, and people. De León earned a BA in Philosophy from Princeton University and a JD from Stanford Law School. She joined NARF in 2017 after judicial clerkships in Alaska and New Jersey and four years at the WilmerHale law firm in Washington, D.C. She is an enrolled member of the Pueblo of Isleta, which is rooted in the Rio Grande Valley near Albuquerque, New Mexico.*

I GREW UP IN Simi Valley, California, north of Los Angeles. It's not a very diverse area, but I would go and visit the reservation with my mom, who is Native, as well as Japanese and Filipino. So from an early age I saw the stark inequities.

At the same time, we had the influence of my dad, who had emigrated from Cuba and was always teaching our family to have a sort of innate love of America. Seeing the way America failed to live up to its ideals, I felt the need to reconcile the inequities I saw with those ideas that we strive for collectively.

My parents had me and my sister when they were young. They then divorced and had more children with their new partners. Between the two families, I have eight brothers and sisters. I guess you can say I've been in a lot of different rooms among a lot of different people. My mom used to call me, "the family policeman." Everyone thought I'd be a lawyer, which is probably one reason why I initially rebelled against the idea.

When I was growing up, I buried myself in achievement. Debate. Rotary. Soccer Captain. Valedictorian. I think a lot of that was trying to prove myself in a community that wasn't particularly diverse. I was an anomaly, obviously different from everybody. so I leaned into making myself exceptional in achievement in order to avoid criticism.

That didn't always protect me. One time my AP History teacher told our class that Native Americans are naturally inclined toward alcoholism. I remember getting in the moment and raising my hand and saying something like, "No! How dare you say that!" Afterwards, my mom marched into the principal's office with me. She wasn't a wilting flower herself.

We demanded a retraction, and the sad and strange thing is that the next day the teacher came in and played the song, "Cherokee Woman." He was trying to explain that he wasn't racist. It was terribly awkward and not very helpful. But what it showed me is that, while he may not have been trying to be quote, unquote "racist," his action and the effect was racism. So I was able at that time to distinguish between how people perceive themselves and what they actually say and do. I experienced that again when I got into several good colleges and an administrator at my high school told me it was only because I was Native American.

At Princeton, De León belonged to a Native American group, but was not, she says, involved in the social justice movement. By the time she graduated she knew she wanted to advocate for Native American rights, but was not sure what form that would take. Back home with her Philosophy degree and a desire to travel, she spent a year as a flight attendant for Alaska Airlines and then applied to law schools. Wait-listed at her top choices, she took a job in Washington, D.C., with the National Congress of American Indians (NCAI) in its policy research center. Then, accepted at Stanford, it was on to law school.

I really loved working at NCAI. I knew I wanted to advocate for Native Americans, and this job was a great primer on understanding not just my own tribal issues, but issues on the national level.

At Stanford, I would characterize myself as being on the track to be a public interest lawyer. I won the first-year law student public interest award, was involved in the Native American Law Students Association and worked at the Supreme Court Clinic.

As I said, I knew I wanted to be involved in the fight for Native American rights, but I didn't go straight into that after graduating from law school. I thought about what to do for a long time and decided the best thing to do was build the credentials that I thought I had to have before pivoting to become an advocate. I think this is a reflection of how I was brought up—to be constantly proving myself. I told myself, *I need to go to law school. And then I need to show that I am objectively a good lawyer.*

So I clerked and then I told myself, *I need to go to a big firm so I can show that I can do this other kind of law so that people understand that I'm a good lawyer. And then I can turn to what I want to do.* I don't think that was necessarily the right way of going about it. But I felt that if I had all of the credentials, then I could give myself permission to do the things that I wanted.

Working at NARF is my dream job. This is what I'm here to do, and I finally feel really validated and happy about it. The wonderful thing about NARF is that we're scrappy. We just come to the issues and do the best that we can. There's such a great need for this work because there are so many disparities.

My focus on voting rights was completely fortuitous, but it's been such an incredible fit in my life. When I arrived at NARF in 2017, my talented former colleague, Natalie Landreth had already put to together a Native American voting rights coalition that included NARF, other voting rights organizations, and some regional organizations. One of the topics that the coalition discussed was why Native Americans don't vote at the same rates as everybody else. And one of my first assignments was to hold a series of field hearings asking the question directly to Indian Country: "Why it is that people aren't voting?" That was such an incredible education on the issues.

In 2017 and 2018, NARF's former pro bono counsel, Jim Tucker, and I held nine hearings in Native communities across the country and heard from about one hundred twenty witnesses. We ultimately wrote a comprehensive, and I think very accessible, report, "Obstacles at Every Turn: Barriers to Political Participation Faced by Native American Voters." Published in June 2020, the report provides detailed evidence that Native people face myriad obstacles in the electoral process: from registering to vote, to casting votes, to having votes counted. I encourage people to go to: vote.narf.org/obstacles-at-every-turn/

During that time I also joined the team working on our North Dakota voter ID case, and then eventually started bringing my own voting rights cases. I also became the lead in our voting rights policy work and ended up testifying several times in the U.S. House and Senate.

The North Dakota case is a good example of the type of work we do. NARF got involved after we heard reports of Native Americans being turned away at the polls. North Dakota had just passed a new ID law directly after the Native vote was instrumental in electing Heidi Heitkamp to the U.S. Senate who won by less than 1 percent. Under the new law, you needed an address on your ID in order to vote. The legislators were well aware that many Native Americans did not have addresses on their homes. Subsequently, qualified American citizens were turned away from voting because they could not show proof of something that they didn't have, nor should they need to have in order to vote.

We spent years compiling that evidentiary record—hiring experts, figuring out how to distill that injustice to one sentence, which is: The State of North Dakota passed a law that required an ID to have an address on it, when they knew that Native Americans did not have addresses on their homes.

Just getting that clarity required a monumental amount of effort, but it demonstrated the mechanisms of discrimination—that in this case it was targeted, was based on race, and that it was in response to a flex of political power. In turn, this record of injustice upset Native communities, and rallied them to get out the vote.

It's an advocacy lawyer's job to tell these complex and difficult stories in an accessible way. There are a lot of steps between that initial investigation and that sentence that crystallizes what's going on.

I'm really proud of the quality of advocacy that comes out of this organization. Right now I am leading voting rights cases and am involved in the push for national voting rights legislation. Last year there was a bipartisan effort to pass the Native American Voting Rights Act, which would remove many of the obstacles to voting that have existed for years. That proposed Act has been incorporated into the Senate's John R. Lewis Voting Rights Act. The voting rights fight has been intense, and NARF continues to advocate for some form of this legislation's passage.

NARF's voting rights work is constantly growing. We've undertaken the largest redistricting project in Indian Country history. We've had our eye on several states, where we are advocating for fairer maps at the local and regional level. We're also pushing against disinformation by getting guides out to those in Indian Country letting them know about their voting rights. We're fighting for the rights of those convicted of felonies to be counted in their home counties when redistricting and allocating resources. We have a project requesting, and at times demanding, counties put polling places on reservations. We are documenting the lack of addressing and disparities in mail delivery services across Indian Country. And, of course, there is always litigation fighting against the laws designed to make it harder for Natives to vote that tend to crop up in places where elections are close and Natives have the potential to control outcomes. It's a constant onslaught, but I love it.

I think there are a lot of ways for one to be an activist or an advocate. There are large and small roles that you can play, personal and public.

For me, it means being a bridge between technical knowledge and in-depth analysis of discrimination and making that knowledge accessible to folks, making it so that people can understand the contours of the injustice so they can rise up against it.

I would say to anyone, "If you have a hunch that something is wrong or unfair, that hunch is probably correct." I think a lot of times folks feel unqualified to make the assessment that they're being wronged or that someone else is being wronged. But trust that instinct. Then take a good look at yourself and figure out what you can contribute—what your place is. There's a role for everybody.

Our gifts can be varied as can our time commitment. Neither of those are disqualifications. It's a big tent, and we need you. There is injustice everywhere. The contribution that you may think is small, can have a large impact.

People have unique gifts. Some people are really good at relating to people. So something as simple as having conversations with some-one about what you think is injustice can be very powerful. Just trust yourself, know yourself, and find opportunities to act.

FOR MORE INFORMATION:
  https://www.narf.org/

'When You're a Point Guard'

RENEE MONTGOMERY, *35, is the co-owner/vice president of the WNBA team, the Atlanta Dream. A native of Charleston, West Virginia, she was a two-time All American and national champion at the University of Connecticut and an All Star and two-time WNBA champion. In June 2020, she opted out of the Dream's WNBA season to be a "catalyst" for social justice reform. She retired as a player in 2021. In addition to her involvement with the Dream, she co-hosts the podcast, "Montgomery & Co."*

AFTER GEORGE FLOYD WAS murdered and the protests began, I was sitting on the couch with my wife, Sirena, and we were looking at the national news, which was talking about what was going on in Atlanta. I'm looking out my window, and I'm looking at the same images that are on tv. I'm in Atlanta! I can see firsthand what's going on. And it was being portrayed in a way that I didn't see or feel. People were trying to make it seem like there was negative energy here, that there was anger. But when I was at the protest, there was a community feel. It felt like people were banding together for a cause.

It was a diverse group. It wasn't only black people. It was black and brown people. There were white people in the protest. It was a whole melting pot. And I thought, *Wow, this is beautiful. I wish people would band together for more causes more times.* And to me, that was the shift. I wanted to add my moment to the momentum. That's why when I opted out of playing for the Dream for the WNBA season in 2020, the tweet that I sent was, "Moments really do equal Momentum." Because I could see all of these different people adding their moment. And I wanted to add mine, too, and join in.

For me, activism means taking the lead with your voice or with your actions and trying to make a change—whatever that change may be. I was raised by leaders, so I think that is where it starts. My dad played football at West Virginia State University, which is where he met my mom, who then became a professor at that same university for thirty years.

Since my parents met at an HBCU, I grew up understanding the value of HBCUs and the underfunding of them and how the system just sometimes cannot do things equally or fairly. But I also grew up seeing black excellence at a very high rate and level.

My mom was in Detroit when the riots took place there in 1967 and '68. She and my dad experienced things that I would think would be a part of our *history,* not a part of our *present*. So when they would tell me these are things that happened to them, you want those things to change at a certain point.

I never aspired to be an activist in the sense of, "Hey, I'm gonna be an activist one day." I didn't even know in 2020 that what I was doing was being an activist. People started giving me that label. And I was like, *What?* To me, it was just speaking up for what I believed in. Speaking about a problem I saw. Speaking up for people that may not even be able to say it themselves.

When people started giving me that title, it made me want to study and learn more. I started to watch different films like Ava DuVernay's documentary, *13th.* I started reading more about the past and talking to different people. I just wanted to understand more.

It was disturbing that a lot of things today were so similar to how they were in the past. You think about how it's 2021 or 2022, and you feel so advanced. Technology is growing at such a rapid rate. And then you look at certain spaces in our society and you're like, *Well, it's too stagnant.* We haven't grown in some areas. You definitely see racism popping up more than it should.

Growing up in the world of athletics, I was outspoken in general.

When you're a point guard, you have to be outspoken because you're the voice on the court. And then to take it a step further, when you get the title of captain, it's not only the voice on the court, but the voice off the court. You're the one that's guiding the team, making sure that everybody stays on track. That's why they give you that title. I've been blessed to be the captain of a majority of the teams that I've been on. I've always taken that role seriously and tried to speak up or tried to do what I considered was right.

I never had to temper what I was saying. I'm very thankful that I went to UConn, where we were able to express ourselves however we saw fit. I can remember when we knew President Obama won in 2008. We were at Coach Auriemma's house and we celebrated. We were able to take joy in the fact that we had our first black president. It was exciting. So I never felt hindered about expressing how I felt. It was even more exciting in 2009, when we won the national championship and were able to go meet him at the White House.

I've always been able to live out loud. Even in broadcasting when I'm calling a basketball game, I call it in a certain style that is my own. The companies that I work for have allowed me to do it. I'm allowed to be my authentic self, even though you don't see a lot of black women in team ownership and sports ownership. You don't see it in those groups, but I'm allowed to still live out loud and be my authentic self.

After opting out of the season, I created the "Remember the 3rd" campaign, which was dedicated to political education and turning out voters in Georgia for the November 3 special election for the U.S. Senate.

No matter what leadership role I take, I never want to feel like I'm telling people what to do. I want people to feel like they are doing what they want to do in their way. That's true at our company, Renee Montgomery Entertainment. It's a creative space. When you think about marketing and creating, you need people to be empowered to make their own choices.

I took that same approach with the Remember the 3rd campaign. I don't want to tell people who to vote for. That's your job to decide who to vote for. However, I do want to educate you on the voting process, educate you on who's available to vote for, educate you on their causes, what they are standing for. I also want you to know that local elections are just as important, if not more important, than national elections. Your local community, that's what builds up our whole national system

Reverend Raphael Warnock eventually won the Senate race, beating the incumbent Kelly Loeffler, who had owned the last team I played on, the Atlanta Dream. Afterward he told ABC, "I think what you were hearing from Renee Montgomery, was that these are not usual times. She felt like she needed to focus on the moment and the rest of the women and the WNBA using that platform, in a way as athletes that recalls the names of Muhammad Ali and John Carlos and others who stood up at the Olympics putting forward a message of justice making in the world." I couldn't believe that we had that big of an impact. "To see the results, it was a surreal moment to have. The WNBA has a place in history," I told ABC.

Some athletes are comfortable with talking to the media. Some athletes are comfortable with giving their personal views, and some aren't. There's a lot that comes with using your voice for a cause. Everybody's not going to agree with how you feel. Everybody's not going to want you to talk about politics or social justice. They might just want you to play basketball. "Shut up and dribble," right? They might just want their favorite athlete to just be their favorite athlete. They don't want to know what their favorite athlete feels off of the court. They just want to know that that that's my favorite athlete and they're good at basketball.

Whenever you decide to tell your views or your opinions out loud, you're putting yourself out there to be judged. You're putting yourself out there to be disliked, because as we know, everybody's going to have a difference in opinions. So it is difficult because you have fans from every different culture. You know that when you make a statement, it's going to offend some fans. But if you understand that what you're saying is your moment and it's needed at that time, then you'll live with that.

In February 2021, Loeffler sold her stake in the team to a three-person investor group that included me. When you think about team ownership and what that typically looks like, it's not a black woman. That to me was one of my main motivations. Representation matters! We talk about that all the time on my podcast, Montgomery and Company, because it's very important that people be able to see what they want to be.

For the podcast, [journalist] Jemele Hill had the vision for us to pivot a little bit. She thought it would be unique if we had black and brown women that were talking about business and culture in addition to sports. That combination is not so common. It wasn't that we were just randomly talking about it. We had credentials. We were talking about the world that we're in. We are in the basketball world, with team ownership; the venture capitalist world. I'm a general partner. We're here, we're immersed. We're in the culture. And so what's different is that we talk about the things that we live and the world we're living in.

There's not very many of us in there. That's the thing that we talk about and that's what we lean into. We try to help people build and grow. We talk to the top business people, we talk to founders, we talk to pro athletes. We've had some pretty amazing guests, including Stacey Abrams.

I always like to encourage people to follow their gut—what it's telling you, what you feel. If you feel like what you're doing is right, then you need to create your own moment. A lot of people think creating their moment needs to be this big grand thing. Creating your own moment can start with just one tweet or with volunteering. It could be anything. So if you're creating your moment and you're adding to the momentum, you're doing something just as much as someone you might see all over TV. Everybody's moment matters.

FOR MORE INFORMATION:
    ReneeMontgomery.net

'I Use the Word Artivist'

LETICIA HERNÁNDEZ-LINARES, *50, is a bilingual, interdisciplinary writer, artist, and racial justice educator. The first-generation U.S.-born daughter of Salvadoran immigrants, she has lived, created, and protested in the Mission District of San Francisco for two decades. She teaches in the College of Ethnic Studies at San Francisco State University.*

AFTER GRADUATING FROM COLLEGE, I got into a PhD program at the University of Pennsylvania in English. Back home in Los Angeles, my family was struggling with economic issues, substance abuse issues, and here I was in a place of privilege. It raised daily questions about my identity as the U.S.-born daughter of immigrants from El Salvador. I realized: *I don't want to be a critic; I want to be the one writing the book and I want to write my stories and I want to write stories for the little girls who were like I had been.*

My parents came to the U.S. as teenagers from El Salvador in 1971. My father was a talented, well-known, musician in his homeland. I was born months after they got here. My first language was Spanish, and I grew up with a really strong sense of who we were, where we were from, and with a strong sense of community.

I didn't have to live through war like my family did, but I did understand it as something that my family experienced. I wanted to find out more because the only source of learning was my father's storytelling and his music as well as movies I found on my own, like *Under Fire* and *Salvador*, which I couldn't get enough of, they were my only mass media entry.

My father collaborated with all kinds of music groups. He was in a Chicano rock band for a long time. There was a lot of activism in East LA. He had Jewish friends, black friends, gay friends. I grew up in a very inclusive environment. There was a sense of socially engaged art and community building that became the lens through which I eventually entered into activism.

My parents struggled a lot in the 1970s and '80s. The first time I went to a predominantly white school—the only time really until college—was in middle school. That was when I learned all of the terrible words that people would use to describe Mexican and Latino people: epithets that communicated: *You don't belong here, you're not worthy, you're not beautiful, you're not valuable.* It was a school that my parents really couldn't afford, but they thought that if they put there, I would get a better education. All It did was turn me off of school and make me not value myself.

Thankfully that was short-lived. I went to high school, where I was a good student. I was so thirsty to learn. But I wasn't a good test taker. I knew I wanted to go to college, but didn't know how to get there. And in those days—even today—most high school guidance counselors directed Latinx kids like me to community college, if college at all.

That's where I started—at community college—but I wanted to go to one of those fancy schools. So I did a lot of research and was accepted at Scripps, one of the Claremont colleges. I couldn't get enough of it. I was like, "This place is so magical. There's so many opportunities, so many resources, so many amazing people, so many great professors. There's the Chicano studies center!"

Black Studies and Chicano Studies saved my life. They made me examine where I was from and what my history here in the United State was. It was an amazing time at Claremont, with an incredible array of scholars and feminists and activists of color, so finding mentors was not difficult.

I had this moment where I asked: "Why the hell did I not know about this?" That was the moment where I said, "I need to make sure that as many other kids who are like me are made aware of these things that are not a given for children of immigrants."

As I said, continuing in the PhD program didn't feel right for me. After becoming disillusioned with the program, I moved to San Francisco. My uncle lived there, and the Mission District had been my happy place growing up. I finished my exams from there to get an MA in English.

I worked as an after school art teacher. The reason I worked after school was because I wanted to create my own curriculum that was bilingual and multicultural; I didn't want to be told what to teach. Lesson planning has been a creative exercise for me since the 1990s—long before Google, a time when you had to figure out how to do or make things on your own.

At the same that I was engaging young people to create a positive experience in the classroom, I started to develop my voice and write more poetry and perform. Since then, I've continued writing and performing my poetry, worked in the nonprofit area, and taught at the college level.

Rather than describe myself as an activist, I use the word "artivist." This is because my community work is so based in my art-making and in my collaboration with other artists and other organizations that I see them as intertwined. You ask yourself what skills and talent you can offer for the greater good. For me, it's wordsmithing, it's teaching, it's communication, having a facility with speaking in front of people and finding joy in performing.

I write about a lot of different things. I come up with ideas for projects that are about evolving my craft, pushing my boundaries and growing as an artist—finding the stories I want to tell, such as stories about the Central American diaspora that need to be made more visible.

When I was a kid, I never read a book about the daughter of immigrants. Later I would learn the problematic history behind the beloved *Little House on the Prairie* books and television series that I used to love and to devour—and realizing who I would have been if I was on that show. It has become important to contest the dominant narrative. It's important to tell stories other than the ones that people want to tell that dehumanize and criminalize a whole people.

Recently I moved into doing installation art, but writing is always at the core of that, or a poem anchors the piece that I create. And it's almost always collaborative. I write about my experiences. I've lived on the same block since 1995 in the Mission, and I've witnessed how displacement has impacted an entire neighborhood, my family, myself.

I have my own stories to write about, but a few years ago I was selected by the Rise-Home Stories Project to write a children's book about gentrification. In 2021, *Alejandria Fights Back! ¡La Lucha de Alejandria!* was published for young readers. It's in English and Spanish and tells the story of a nine-year-old girl whose family and neighbors face displacement and who uses her voice to fight back. It's illustrated by Rob Liu-Trujillo and translated by Dr. Carla España.

The action in the book was inspired by my son, who when he was nine stood up at a historic preservation commission meeting to speak on behalf of one of our community artist centers that was facing eviction. In the book, the mother resembles my mother. She aims not to make trouble and relies on just keeping her head down to stay below the radar. There's a lot of the thinking around being a renter—the idea that you have to just be good and not bother your landlord. But, no! You deserve to live in a clean, safe home without fear. You deserve to live in your community, with your neighbors, in a place that you call home.

The Rise-Home Stories Project describes itself as a "groundbreaking collaboration between multimedia storytellers and social justice advocates seeking to change our relationship to land, home, and race, by transforming the stories we tell about them." In addition to my book, other artists have created a narrative driven video game, a nonfiction podcast, an animated web series, and an interactive online experience.

I've taught Latina,Latino Studies, Race and Resistance Studies, and Gender and Women's Studies at San Francisco State. What I tell my students and teachers that I train to develop an anti-racist teaching practice, and to the young kids that I teach poetry workshops to is this: "Investigate and celebrate who you are and where you come from. That starts just with your name. Demand that your name be pronounced the way your mother sings it at home."

That's been a lifelong battle for me and now for my sons who have trilingual names. It really shouldn't threaten anyone that I ask for my name to be said, Leticia (Le-tee-cee-a), as opposed to (Letisha). That's just not my name. I can't tell you the book I could write about the experiences I've had with that single thing. So it's important knowing who you are, having a sense of where you come from, what your relationship is to the community or the world or your surroundings.

From there it's asking what's the change you want and why. What's your stake in it? For me, it's very related to my own personal struggles and education as a first generation citizen here in the United States. After that, it's doing research, finding out what's already happening, who's been out there doing it, who can you learn from.

I'm finally living that dream of a world that nobody could shape and that you don't need a PhD to be in. Doing the thing that feels right in your gut, that's the best reward.

Here's an excerpt from my poem, "On the First Day of War, I'm Supposed to Teach Poetry":

Crumpled flyers hold up letters curling into small fists.
Declaring for fill in the blank geographic locations.
U.S. OUT OF . . .
Countries stand single file down the page. Long list of wrong time
wrong place nations pushing and shoving for their recognition
in the blank of t-shirt or button slogan. Like the ones teaching me
about back home, my points of reference: war broadcasts
and loud voices over a delayed signal. Long distance phone calls

hung over my childhood like a rain cloud moving. Rain back home, my father would relate, came warm from the sky and traveled as if it were running.

FOR MORE INFORMATION:

joinleticia.com

risehomestories.com

Alejandria Fights Back/Alejandria defiende 2021

Wandering Song: Central American Writing in the United States, edited by Leticia Hernández-Linares, Rubén Martínez, Héctor Tobar, 2017.

Mucha Muchacha, Too Much Girl, 2015.

Razor Edges of My Tongue. 2002.

'Uplifting the Underrepresented'

CHEICK CAMARA, *21, and* ERMIAS TADESSE, *22, cofounded BlackGen Capital, Inc., a minority-owned investment fund, in 2019 while they were undergraduates at Cornell University. Each currently works in the investment banking community in New York. BlackGen seeks to close the access gap by creating a pipeline for talented, underrepresented students interested in entering the financial services industry.*

CHEICK: Ermias and I were in some of the organizations at Cornell that provided different resources to help students learn about finance and provide opportunities to connect with employers on Wall Street. Our "moment" was just looking around the room and seeing there was no representation of people of color. We realized that there was definitely a disconnect between those running the organizations and the group that needed these resources the most—people who looked like us.

ERMIAS: I came to Virginia from Ethiopia when I was five. My family has always been involved in community service—helping out at food pantries, cooking for our church, driving people to church. My parents are my role models, and their tradition of helping the people around them inspired me to continue on to that same mission. I was involved in the Salvation Army from the age of seven until I graduated high school. The volunteering that I did mostly revolved around homelessness.

CHEICK: I grew up in East Harlem. I learned the act of selflessness from my mom, who emigrated from Bamako, Mali. She's a single mother who struggled with finances at times, but just worked really hard to make ends meet. Her example inspired me to be an activist, which I'd define as someone who is a catalyst for change, a voice for the voiceless, a person that's able to take action for those who can't take actions for themselves. Activists work with the mentality that if they don't solve these issues then nobody else will.

I went to a public high school in the South Bronx, that didn't have many resources. I founded an SAT Math club because I was fortunate enough to get some good resources from an external program. So every week I would tutor kids from three different schools.

ERMIAS: To me activism is trying to find a solution to problems by bringing people together and making sure that everyone is included in resolving that problem.

CHEICK: I've always been entrepreneurial. In elementary school, I started a candy business with a loan of twenty dollars from my mom. I went to Target, bought packs of Fruit Snacks and resold that to friends in fifth grade. Fast forward to high school, I continued with different endeavors such as reselling sneakers.

When I got to Cornell, I wanted to be a doctor. I think that was because of pressures from my immigrant parents. They didn't have exposure to any other careers. In their minds, the only way to be successful is if you become a doctor or lawyer. They didn't know about finance or Wall Street. I think my counterparts from affluent backgrounds have this exposure earlier on. When I got to Cornell, I got the exposure through different finance clubs and eventually realized this is a career I can do and pursue. But as I said, there was no one at these clubs who looked like me—except Ermias.

ERMIAS: I also came to Cornell pre-med. My parents wanted me to be a doctor so they pushed me to study biology. I enjoyed the classes, but I knew it wasn't for me. In high school I was also involved in various entrepreneurship organizations. I really liked the idea of building an idea and a product and being able to market and sell that to consumers. Same as Cheick, my parents had no idea what Wall Street was, what finance was and the opportunities that exist within it. So once I learned the fact that I can create generational wealth in this industry, I fully pursued that.

Because the organizations we were in didn't fully connect to people like us, Cheick and I were inspired to create BlackGen Capital in 2019. It's a student investment fund focused specifically on uplifting underrepresented minorities and providing them access to education resources such as financial literacy, investing and just all of the tools that we believe are crucial for building things like generational wealth, closing the financial access gap that exists in America, and also allowing them to break into these prestigious careers on Wall Street that they previously were denied access to. We offer a ten-week course that outlines accounting, finance, financial literacy, and investment analysis.

CHEICK: In creating BlackGen our first step was to establish the vision and mission. What are we going to stand for as an organization? How are we going to solve the existing problems on our campus and across the country? After that it was a matter of establishing more of the foundational and the framework things such as culture. When we do bring on teammates, how do we want to work together and work towards the same mission? Culture is key. Then it was recruiting teammates for the initial founding board. We needed to make sure that everyone had complementary skill sets, and we could each kind of bounce off of each other.

ERMIAS: Our culture stems from our core values, which are diversity, empowerment, education, and philanthropy. Inclusivity is key. When we advertise BlackGen Capital to the students, we emphasize that no prior finance experience is needed. You just have to come in with a passion and with an eagerness to collaborate with other students. We know that we also lacked that access in the past, so we don't want to block out any students.

We emphasize that everything revolves around teamwork. So our students do stock pitches in their own separate teams where they work with students across all different grade levels, different majors, to produce a pitch that they present to the entire organization at the end of the semester. That's how we choose our fund's investments.

We now have an established fund that we worked for about two years to set up. We raised money through corporate sponsors we solicited with formal presentations, like Bank of America, Bloomberg, Morgan Stanley. These big institutional firms really want to diversify their workforces, so they partner with us to tap into our diverse talent. In exchange they help us raise funds. We've raised around sixty thousand dollars so far, and that's just going to continue to grow as we get more corporate sponsors.

CHEICK: Beyond the investments, BlackGen emphasizes philanthropy. We donate some of our profits to make sure that we're giving back to black and Latinx owned businesses. We realized that this not just about BlackGen or about us. It's really a lot more than that, and hopefully this can be a catalyst for so much more change.

ERMIAS: We also want to make sure that once we graduate that BlackGen stays at Cornell and continues to expand across the nation. In addition to our chapter, we have a chapter at Georgetown University. Cheick and I along with a team of three students are working as a national board and sort of overseeing our chapters and our expansion. Once we all graduate, we plan to hand over the keys to the next presidents and board and make sure that they just keep it going. Some day we might even expand to high schools.

I think it's very easy to underestimate the power of mentorship to help a person or an organization succeed. It's just the power of having someone more senior than you guide you throughout college and throughout any endeavor you want to take, because you definitely don't want to be making the same mistakes that someone else made. Once you get to college, a new place, having a junior or senior to help guide you through it allows you to leverage their experiences to mature yourself in that environment. Finding a mentor is 100 percent my tip to anyone who wants to be an activist.

CHEICK: A couple of other things: If you're a young person who sees a problem, you should know that if you don't solve it, then no one else will. You cannot be passive and wait for somebody else to step up. You've got to make sure to take that initiative. When Ermias and I cofounded BlackGen, we wondered why something like this hadn't existed for decades. It's because people noticed the issue, but they were just looking for other people to actually take that initiative and solve it.

I think another thing is really being receptive to feedback and being involved in diagnosing whatever solution you're working on—making sure that it's an actual solution. Analyzing it to determine what are the ways to constantly improve it. The first attempt is never going to be perfect, so it's all about iteration and making sure that you can improve on it over and over.

ERMIAS: After graduation I began working full-time at Goldman Sachs in their investment banking division.

CHEICK: I'm now working at Evercore Partners in the investment banking division.

ERMIAS: I think our parents are excited. As I said, this is something that's completely new to them. When I told them that I would be an investment banker out of college, they had no idea what that was. They assumed that it was the equivalent to a bank teller at your local bank. That shows you how underexposed our community really is.

FOR MORE INFORMATION:
www.blackgencapital.com

'Having a Spiritual Life'

RABBI JILL JACOBS, *46, is CEO at New York City–based T'ruah: The Rabbinic Call for Human Rights. T'ruah seeks to protect and advance social justice by training and mobilizing its network of two thousand rabbis and cantors, together with their communities, to bring Jewish values to life through strategic and meaningful action.*

I WENT TO A big public high school in a suburb of Boston in the early 1990s. It was a pretty conservative place, mostly Catholic. Our principal was quoted in the local paper as saying that there was no teen pregnancy problem at the school. I thought that he was probably wrong, so I started doing some research of my own. I found out that not only did we have one of the highest rates of teen pregnancy in Massachusetts, we also had one of the highest rates of STDs. We were also one of only two or three schools in the entire state that had zero sex education whatsoever, and this seemed relevant.

This was during the height of the AIDS epidemic, which solidified the fact that this lack of education was a matter of life or death. I quickly got together with some friends and we started a petition to have condoms available in our school, to have sex education, and to have reading materials available to students. We knew it was a long shot for all of these asks, but we actually were successful in bringing sex education into the school.

I grew up in a Conservative family that kept kosher and went to synagogue regularly. I attended Hebrew school, was active in youth groups, and continued to be immersed in Jewish life throughout my upbringing. But I wasn't raised in a home or a Jewish community that was particularly activist. People were liberal Democrats, but I don't have early memories of going to protests or doing other kinds of advocacy. We might go to the soup kitchen once a year on Christmas to volunteer, or put coins in a box, or donate cans of food, but our advocacy did not go beyond these basic actions.

I started to become more active during high school, but never consciously connected that activism to my Judaism. I had no idea that Jewish women were at the forefront of reproductive rights struggles for years, yet it was clear to me that what I was doing was at least acceptable within my Jewish community. I had a nascent sense that something in Judaism supported this kind of activism.

After high school, I attended Columbia University, looking for an observant Jewish community and an activist campus. At that point, I wasn't planning on becoming a rabbi. The rabbis I knew at the time were all middle-aged men. But Columbia was only six blocks south of the Jewish Theological Seminary (JTS), and when I would go there for services, I saw rabbinical students who were close to my age, both men and women. It suddenly seemed possible that I could actually be a rabbi, too.

I'd heard fantasy stories about Columbia in the 1960s—full of sit-ins and protests. That was certainly not Columbia in the 1990s. My first year, I started to learn about worker justice when the administrative workers on campus went on strike. But still, for me, the Jewish community work and the social justice work were two parallel paths. I didn't know how to bring them together.

My thinking really changed when I got to JTS in 1998. Like Columbia, the seminary is in the middle of Harlem, where I had lived since moving to New York. After years of living in the neighborhood, I decided that I had to know what was actually happening there, so I went looking for a place to get involved.

I found myself volunteering with an organization that was working on housing issues in central Harlem. It was a ten-minute walk between its office and JTS. Yet, when I would walk there and walk back, it was like two different worlds. When I was in Harlem, people would say, "Wow, you're the first Jew I've ever met who's not a slum lord." And when I was at JTS, people would say, "Are you sure that it's safe there?"

I wanted to figure out how these worlds could come together. I wondered if any scholars in the history of Judaism had ever talked about housing, and I soon found myself focusing on a chapter of *Talmud* in which, fifteen hundred years ago, the rabbis talked about when you're allowed to evict somebody and when you're not. For example, you can't evict people during the winter when housing is hard to find and it's dangerous to be outside.

I was surprised to learn that ancient Jewish tradition actually had something to teach about modern housing conditions. That led me to an exploration of several ancient Jewish texts about housing and labor issues. I found over and over that these texts had insights and real wisdom to share that connected to the injustices I was seeing in the present day. That realization set me on the path that has led me to currently lead a rabbinic human rights organization.

In my last year at JTS, I was determined to find work in social justice after graduating, but at that point, Jewish social justice wasn't a field in the way that it is today. Nevertheless, I got lucky and found a job in Chicago as Director of Outreach and Education at the Jewish Council on Urban Affairs, whose goal is to involve the Jewish community to advance racial and economic justice. Two-and-a- half years later, I came back to New York to serve as the rabbi-in-residence for another organization, Bend the Arc [formerly Jewish Funds for Justice], devoted to engaging the Jewish Community in the fight for social justice.

By this point I had been doing mostly domestic justice work—U.S. only—professionally, but really wanted to think about what it meant to be involved in Israel as well, as I had been during rabbinical school. I was accepted into the Jerusalem Fellows, a program that the Mandel Institute in Jerusalem then ran for mid-career Jewish educators. I spent most of my time working on a book about how to do social justice within the Jewish community, including questions of one's relationship to place, including Israel.

I realized that I could no longer work only on domestic issues. I quit my job, finished my book, and then—in what can be described as *bashert* [destiny], T'ruah, was looking for its next executive director. I got the job and started in April 2011. We're still the only organization in the Jewish social justice sphere in the U.S. that has a commitment to working 50 percent on domestic issues and 50 percent on Israel. I was not interested in giving up working on U.S.-based issues, but also have a commitment to changing the situation in Israel, to ensure the human rights of both Israelis and Palestinians.

In the U.S, our main issues include mass incarceration and police reform, immigration, and worker justice, with a focus on the supply chain on slavery and trafficking. We also believe that a just and secure future for Israelis and Palestinians will best be achieved by a negotiated resolution that results in both peoples living within their own sovereign states. We advocate for an end to the military occupation of the West Bank and Gaza and an end to the continued expansion of the settlements that extend this occupation. And we affirm Israel's existence as a homeland for Jews.

We've been working on these issues for at least the past ten years or more—sometimes all twenty years of our existence, such as in the case of fighting occupation. We'd rather do a few things well than do a lot of things not so well. But when there is either a possibility of taking on a new campaign or changing direction on a campaign, we go through a staff and board process and ask questions like: Is this a Jewish issue? Is this a human rights issue? How do we talk about this in a Jewish way? Is this a place where we feel like we can have a unique contribution?

Our work in addressing mass incarceration and police reform demonstrates how we fulfill our mission. First, we affirm unequivocally that black lives matter. We take a human rights approach to our work, as we always do, including: advocating for an end to police practices that result in disproportionate stops, arrests, and deaths of people of color; organizing rabbis and their communities to protest police violence and to demand full investigations in cases of killings by police officers; advocating for more just sentencing policies; organizing to end prolonged solitary confinement; and giving Jewish communities the education and background they need to do work locally, including volunteering with incarcerated individuals and their families, employing the formerly incarcerated, and engaging in local campaigns to change state criminal justice laws.

What I am seeing now is a whole generation of young Jews who very much want to connect their Jewish life to their activist life. That shows up in lots of different ways, including through building Jewish communities. Maybe it's in a synagogue, or maybe it's just having Shabbat dinner with friends who also do activism. You might be singing a Jewish song at your protest, or you might be participating in a demonstration that coincides with Pesach and raises themes of liberation, or you might be bringing justice into your seder. You're going to connect your Jewish ritual life and your Jewish spiritual life to your activism. They're not two separate things.

In choosing how and where to focus one's activism, I would say, first, learn about the issue that's bothering you and find out who is working on it. Sometimes there's this feeling that anybody who has an idea should start an organization or start a project or start a company, but very often there are people who have been working on whatever it is for longer perhaps than many of us have been alive. Maybe there are people in your neighborhood who have been working on this for fifty years and have a lot of experience and expertise and ideas, and maybe the best thing is to be of service to that organization or that project. Maybe you still have a lot to learn from people closest to the injustice, and you should ask how your efforts can lift up and support those voices.

It's also important to understand that if you're doing an internship or you're volunteering, the work might not be very glamorous, and it might not feel like it's the important work—but it is important. It might be stuffing envelopes or babysitting during an organizing meeting. It might not feel like, *oh, this is exciting activism*. But I think, particularly for people who are just getting involved, it's important to take our cues from the community and to figure out what it is that we can do to be of service—and also not to assume that we have the answers or just need to start something immediately.

We also have examples where young people in particular, because of their excitement and commitment, are able to draw attention to an issue in ways that older people haven't. The climate movement and March for Our Lives are prime examples, where the voices of young people saying, "Hey, we want to live," got such well-deserved attention.

There are places where it's about finding your peers and organizing, yet everyone should understand that fighting for social justice is long and hard work. There are good, quick victories, but more often there are not.

We have to commit to be in this fight for the long run, which also means that we can't burn ourselves out along the way. Having a connection to a spiritual community is helpful because that's part of what gives us the resilience to be able to keep going for the long term. Having a spiritual practice including Shabbat can help build this resiliency. This forces us to take one day when we're not trying to change the world around us; one day when we're saying, "Actually I can't do everything."

FOR MORE INFORMATION:
Truah.org
Books by Rabbi Jill Jacobs:
There Shall Be No Needy (2009)
Where Justice Dwells (2011)

'We'll Grow Food'

DAZMONIQUE CARR, *27, is a food educator, food grower, founder of Deeply Rooted Produce, Detroit's First Zero Waste mobile grocery store which delivers fresh, affordable, locally sourced fruits and vegetables to Detroiters. She is also co-owner of Detroit's first farm-to-table corner store.*

I WENT TO WAYNE State University (WSU) in Detroit on a track scholarship. When I was there, I started learning more about nutrition and how eating the right foods can fuel your body to be a better athlete and healthier in general.

I started volunteering with the Biodiversity Network, a student organization that grew different Michigan native plants. I didn't know anything about Michigan natives, but I knew I was food insecure and I could barely afford the food that was at the grocery store across the street.

I was, like, *I need to grow food for myself.* So I started volunteering at Keep Growing Detroit. They exposed me to Earthworks Urban Farm on the east side of the city, which had a nine-month training program that taught you everything from seed to table. You are in the ground on their two-and-a-half-acre farm learning everything from A to Z. From that I learned it was so important to take a two dollar pack of seed and turn that into an abundance of food. And that was self-sufficiency.

I grew up in Lawnside, New Jersey, a small, historically black town. My dad has always been involved in helping people, selflessly. Same thing with my mom. She has been in education all her life and is currently a nurse. I started volunteering when I was five or six.

Activism was one of the principles I learned as a Girl Scout, and I did volunteer work when I was in high school to get scholarships. I volunteered with the homeless and always asked why our society was doing what it was doing. A mentor encouraged me to start educating myself, and I learned that there were a lot of things that needed to be changed or improved.

I always knew I would be helping someone. My mom wanted me to be a teacher—and I am a teacher in certain realms of life now—but I started out to be a personal trainer or physical therapist before developing my interest in food and nutrition. Once I kicked out the meat from my diet and just focused on fruits and vegetables that I got from the farm, I was hooked on the fact that I could grow my own food—didn't have to rely on other entities to secure my food.

The first place I grew anything on my own was at a community garden on the west side of Detroit. It's part of a not-for-profit called Auntie Na's House. Auntie Na herself is a pillar of the community whose outreach includes after school programs, help with employment and housing, and feeding the hungry. You can go there for community meals. She had about six parcels, totaling about half an acre.

Auntie Na allowed me to just flow, do whatever I wanted to. I donated some of what I grew to her, took home food for myself, and anything that I didn't eat, I would sell. That's what a lot of farmers do. They start out growing for their household and then it's like, *Oh, wow, I have an abundance.* And then it's, *Well, I don't want this to go to waste.* So they'll either donate it or try to sell it.

During my junior year at WSU, I created Students Feeding Students, where we provided healthy food we either grew or was donated to students and staff. Eventually I started a mobile grocery store. I would ride my bike with a basket on the back full of produce; that was my mobile distribution! Then I replaced the bike with a little wagon to carry watermelons and containers of other produce because they were too heavy for the bike.

Farming wasn't completely foreign to me. Both my dad and my

mother grew up near Elizabethtown, North Carolina. Each of their families had an acre or two reserved for growing food for the household. My dad and my mother grew up with chickens in their backyard, and when I was younger, I watched my uncles kill chickens or just chase chickens and collect eggs. I didn't understand it then, didn't value it. But I was still there. It was still a picture in my head that that was going on and that was what was needed to survive and be self-sufficient.

At about the same time I was growing food at Auntie Na's, I signed up for a business training program at ProsperUs Detroit, which describes itself as, "an economic development initiative that builds and sustains neighborhood entrepreneurs and small businesses." There were a lot of chefs there that were revamping their food businesses, and I began to sell to them and some local farmer's markets. My residential business started picking up, too .

2017 was a big year. I graduated from college, officially registered my business—Deeply-Rooted LLC (Deeply Rooted Produce)—with the state, and bought my first vehicle. Since then we've continued to supply restaurants and grocery stores, sold at farmers markets, and grown our residential business. I have five parcels of my own land now, but the business primarily acts as a wholesaler, selling the produce of local farmers. We sell subscription boxes—community supported agriculture (or CSA) boxes—where people get a weekly or biweekly box from us of different produce from different farmers.

I knew that different people just like me were growing the food, but it's hard to grow the food, harvest the food, pack it up for market, and then there's no guaranteed sale. So I wanted to be able to have the guaranteed sale that you get when people purchase subscriptions. We're really promoting a local economy by getting the food these farmers grow to customers. And then the customers have local food that has been grown near them.

We work with a lot of Detroit black-owned and -operated farms. About 80 percent of the produce that we source is from Detroit farmers, most of whom are located on the east side of the city. The other 20 percent is mainly from white farmers in Western Michigan.

Our Detroit farming partners have parcels of varying sizes, from half an acre to one that I've seen that is only fifty feet by one hundred feet. Some of these farmers have more than one lot. The five parcels that I own are adjacent to my house. Some owners have up to thirty lots, so their total might be two to seven acres.

It's very hard for these farmers to farm full-time. Unless you are distributing large amounts of food, it's very hard to make livable margins. A lot of the farmers are really good at growing food, but not too good at growing or operating their business. I've seen many farmers struggle, and that's where Deeply Rooted Produce is coming in: to help with the business side of things, the distribution, the farmer's markets.

The farmers just have to grow the food and harvest it. We buy wholesale, whole units from different farmers so that they have a consistent income. We do Sunday dinners, so that the food that otherwise wouldn't have been going into produce boxes will go into a dinner once a week for the community at a donation base. So we're still buying produce from the farmers, but now the community has different ways to access that food as well. Because there are people that are food insecure, too. We're also teaching healthy eating habits and food preparation.

There are a lot of grocery stores in Detroit that are not owned and operated by Detroiters. And so they don't have an understanding for the food that Detroiters may or may not consume. Also the quality of food is often terrible and it's overpriced. We believe there are over 157,000 liquor stores and party stores in the city versus only seven privately owned grocery stores.

I've gone through a lot of programs to learn how to run a business and have gained networks to help along the way. In 2021 I gained a business partner, Rafael Wright, who is hoping to open a community-funded grocery store called Neighborhood Grocery, which will be a brick and mortar store, Detroit's only black-owned grocery store.

We're partnering so that Deeply Rooted is the wheels aspect of the store. We'll grow food on his land that will go both to Deeply Rooted and to the store.

My brain is always churning and turning. I'm a visionary. I have a lot of different detailed visions in regards to how I would like things to go for me in the future. I just learn from experience; I learn from doing. If I had never planted a seed and was too nervous or never did anything, I wouldn't be where I am today, five years later.

Once you figure out there's a problem that you actually have the capacity to help out with, do something. Don't just wait for someone else to come in and magically snap their fingers and fix it. There are many different neighborhoods that are perceived to be run down—purposefully so in some areas. There are different ways that we can plant trees and plant little bushes to beautify these areas. There are programs in cities like Detroit where you can claim that lot. And now you're a parcel owner. You're a real estate owner.

So my advice is get involved, no matter how small you think what you're doing is—If it's packing up sandwiches for the homeless, or if it's something along the lines of helping someone younger, because it's always important to look back and educate those that are younger than you.

In the African diaspora, there is the story of the Sankofa bird, whose head is looking backwards as it carries a precious egg forward. The proverb that goes with it says, "It is not wrong to go back for that which you have forgotten." That can be anything, including yourself.

One must be patient with theirself and definitely learn and grow from their mistakes. People spend a lot of time praying and pleading for help, and they don't realize that the process that they're in is a prayer that they most likely asked for. One must learn to appreciate the process and must really be in tune with self and figure out what self wants and what self needs. Because, honestly, I think once we realize who we are and we realize what power lies within self, that's when we succeed.

There are so many different lessons, but the one lesson I'm being intentional about right now is figuring out myself. We can take in so many different things from the world and from other people, who make us think we should care about this or do that. But sit down by yourself. Meditate. Think. Pray. That's when you can really figure out the things you care about and want to do.

FOR MORE INFORMATION:
deeplyrootedproduce.com
neighborhood-grocery.com
Instagram: @deeplyrootedproduce @neighborhoodgrocery
@criterionurbanfarm @sisters_on_a_roll_mobile_cafe
@asameansdoctor @magcreatedit
@makethehoodgreatagain @rivendellgardensllc
@pillarpride @rescuenaturenow @keepgrowingdetroit
@tastediasporadetroit @brothernatureproduce

'Involved in Community Medicine'

DAVID MATA, 33, will graduate from the Loyola University Chicago Stritch School of Medicine in 2023. Undocumented and active in the fight for immigrant rights, he plans to practice community medicine in low-resourced areas. He received an Albert Schweitzer Fellowship for 2020–2021 from the Chicago-based Health and Medicine Policy Research Group.

MY MOM AND I were sitting on the couch watching the news and there were reports of all these things happening to migrants, to undocumented youth, and undocumented families. They were being arrested, deported, separated. And my mom said to me, "I wish we could do something."

This was around 2010, a couple of years before DACA. I was in college and undocumented myself. When she said that, instead of just sitting on the couch, watching the news. I said, "You know what, Mom? We *can* do something."

I think that's when it all started for me. That's when I said, "I want to get involved. This isn't fair." My family was going through this. Many of my friends and their families were in the same circumstance. That's kind of where it started taking off.

I grew up in Holland, Michigan, a home to many migrants and farm workers. My family is originally from Mexico. I moved to the United States when I was six years old. It wasn't until my senior year in high school that I discovered I was undocumented. I was filling out my college applications and there was a little block that said "Social Security Number," and I was like, *I don't know what my number is. I'll just ask my parents. It's not a big deal.*

When I got home I said, "Mom, I need these numbers for college."
And she said, "You don't have any."
And I said, "What do you mean I don't?"

This was 2005. DACA and the opportunity to have some sort of legal status was seven years away. Imagine this: I'm applying to college with a dream of becoming a doctor, and I'm now thinking that I can't go. I had two full-ride scholarships that were taken away due to my undocumented status. It was a very scary time. I got really desperate to find opportunities, and I called our state representatives. Unfortunately, we lived in a very conservative area of the state, so they weren't very sympathetic or helpful. But, I managed to figure it out. I called the Mexican embassy, and was told, "You can go to these universities and be charged a regular in-state tuition, just like everyone else in the state, not an unfair and obscene international rate tuition." And I was able to go to school.

Unfortunately, those challenges never really went away. Even today, although I'm now a permanent resident, my family is still undocumented. Individuals like me may have adjusted status or have some sort of legal status such as DACA that is under control of the governing party, but we still have our families, and our families are still being broken. I have family members in Mexico who are aging. I can go see them, but my parents can't see them. My mom just missed her own mother's funeral last year. My dad has lost his grandparents. My family has not been reunited for more than twenty-five years. So just because I'm fine, status-wise, doesn't mean our community is fine.

After I told my mom that we could do something, I slowly began looking for organizations that were aligned with what I wanted to do, which was to speak out for immigration rights. But before that even, the first step was to determine that I was comfortable in my own skin; I now call that "pride." I didn't use to call it that, but, yeah, I am undocumented and it has shaped me into the person that I am. I've grown as a person because of the experiences that I've lived through. There is so much power in our self-acceptance.

So for anyone wanting to put themselves out there, I think it's first being comfortable. Because if you aren't comfortable in your own skin, with your own status and your own vulnerabilities, it's really hard to put forward this strong persona to talk about certain issues.

I thank my parents for modeling the activist behavior that gave me the courage and values. They always said to be a good person, be a person for your community, help people out. If you speak English, help someone who doesn't speak it. Stand up for them when no one else will.

The most notable organization I found was Michigan United, a social justice group that grew out of the merger of the Michigan Organizing Project and the Alliance for Immigrant Rights. They were the first ones that put me out there to speak.

I spoke to students at various universities. I spoke with state and federal representatives. I spoke with the mayor, our university president. I did live interviews on TV and radio. It was scary. Looking back I'm so proud to have been part of that first cohort of fearless pre-DACA, undocumented individuals. I remember one speech I gave in particular. We were in a park, and there were policemen all around the perimeter. As soon as I saw them, my voice started cracking. It felt like the words weren't coming out—because I was scared, you know. The police was literally right there, and they could have deported me at any time.

I still remember my friend Gina's mom that day. She was in the front row and she was crying just looking at me with hope. It just reminded me that I was speaking for them, for those too scared to speak. So I got that strength back, and I was able to finish what I was saying. I look back at it and think, *Wow, I was fearless. How did I muster that courage to do that?* But that was part of my growth as a person and development of my guiding philosophy. I realized I had an inherent quality to advocate for others, whether it's my community, my family, my friends, my classmates. I knew whatever I did would involve speaking out fearlessly for change.

I graduated from college in 2010, pre-DACA. So I was stuck

education-wise. I had a degree, but couldn't go to medical school because of my status. I worked in a restaurant, which was weird, but okay. Then the university changed its policy and accepted undocumented students to graduate programs. So I got a Master's degree in Biology. Then DACA happened in 2012. I felt unstoppable and I decided to apply to medical school.

Unfortunately, with other responsibilities—teaching, defending my thesis, publishing a paper—I didn't do well on the MCAT and didn't get in to medical school. I moved to Chicago and for the next five years did public health. I got to work with communities that were very different than the ones I'd worked in when living in western Michigan. My first research project involved surveying and treating depression and anxiety in older adults. Then I was involved with community health workers in a project to reduce diabetes disparities in socioeconomically disadvantaged populations. After that I helped design a program for the prevention of lead paint poisoning in kids.

I was fortunate to find a mentor in Dr. Steve Rothschild, the chair of Family Medicine at Rush University Medical Center. He led volunteer trips abroad to provide medical services, and I went on one to the Dominican Republic. He's really into community-centered assessments, something that has influenced my way of approaching things. I learned from him—and others, too—an approach to developing relationships with patients. It's very frequently not how much you know; it's how much you listen to them, try to understand them, trying to meet them halfway, and advocating for them. He set such a powerful example for me in the type of physician I wanted to be.

I applied to medical schools again and am now completing my third year at Loyola University Chicago Stritch School of Medicine. I know I want to work in low-resourced areas. I'd love to be a professor who teaches community programs or community-based health—giving that personal touch to these classes and mentoring students.

A couple of years ago I applied for a fellowship with HMPRG in

Chicago [Health and Medicine Policy Research Group]. My proposed project was to work with LGBTQ homeless youth in the Humboldt Park area at a predominantly Latino and black shelter. I wanted to give them self-sufficiency workshops so they could live more independent lives. Unfortunately COVID put an end to that.

Instead, all of us fellowship recipients did what was needed at the moment. I helped develop a bilingual curriculum that prepared about four hundred community health workers to go out and educate the community on COVID. Then I did a COVID intervention curriculum so high school students would have the confidence to teach their classmates, their parents or their neighbors on how to be better prepared for COVID.

I know I want to be involved in community medicine, and I hope to continue telling my own story. Personal narratives humanize experience. My parent didn't even finish middle school. They were farm workers, factory workers. These are the people that carried me through college and through medical school. I remember my dad at one point was working three jobs just so he could pay for my education and for my brother's. That's my story.

I can describe the qualities of an activist better than I can define "activist." An activist is always fearless, speaks for the people that are frequently silenced. Activists hold their ground. They have to be resilient, be used to constantly being told "no," but willing to keep going.

But go at your own pace. Change takes forever. Even after DACA, we had to keep advocating two or three more years until Michigan allowed driver licenses to us. It took a very, very long time.

My mom is my hero. And one of her mantras translated into English is, "What's the rush?" When I didn't get into medical school, she said, "What's the rush?" So I tell people to be patient. I also tell them you can't save the world. I wish I could advocate for all of the things that I'm really passionate about, but I can't do that. So I've focused my advocacy on healthcare and the communities that I want to serve.

Whatever you decide, get the confidence to be an advocate by first speaking to your friends and family about really controversial issues that you're really passionate about. Then after you get practiced doing it with your peers, start going above and beyond that. Join organizations that align with the things that you believe in. Work your way up to being the leader that you want to be.

I think it's also really important not to burn out, to know when to take a step back. This process is not easy. When it comes to advocacy, it's very easy to feel discouraged. It's very easy to want to give up. That's when a team comes in. That's when having a community approach is so important. My colleagues reinvigorate me. Like-minded people reinvigorate me. The community reinvigorates me.

I frequently ask myself: why do I keep getting up? And the answer is: it's always just seeing the injustices to people and seeing the unfairness that people face.

FOR MORE INFORMATION:
www.hmprg.org

'We Started in the Schools'

KEITH WHITE, 46, *is a legal expert and community advocate who cofounded the not-for-profit community organization, Brooklyn Combine, which works with schools, community organizations, and city officials in New York to help provide critical education, leadership, and social support programs to youth and young adults in low-income and underserved communities.*

I LEFT MY JOB as a prosecutor in the DA's office, and I said, "Okay. I want to try to make some money to support my family." And so I was two years out of law school, in private practice and running around practicing in various areas, and I made costly mistakes. I did some things the wrong way, and as a result my license to practice law was suspended for two years.

And during that time, I was like, *Well, who am I?* That was my moment: asking myself, *Who am I?* And in that moment I thought: *Am I holding on to this capitalist creed? Am I doing this thing where I'm trying to be the richest guy? Or do I really care about all of the things that I pretended to care about when I was in law school, coming up?* And so that was the moment for me where I said, "I'm going back to practicing law, and I'm going to go back in a way where I'm actually doing the things that are in alignment with my real value systems. Where there's no distinction between who I am on an everyday basis." And that was it for me.

I was born and raised in the Brownsville section of Brooklyn. In my home, there was no activist or advocate ethic. It was: work hard, mind your business, keep your head down, and get a civil servant job because that's how you survive in this country. That, or join a union. That was kind of the ethic for much of my childhood. But it came into conflict with my studies when I was in college from 1994 to 1998.

In college I was aware of instances where people of color who were actually minding their business were still subject to abject violence. I didn't experience physical violence, but was subjected to violence in the form of silence, disparity, inequity, those things. So I started to ask myself questions. *Am I really supposed to kind of accept this as okay? And even if I can be well-adjusted to these inequities, what about someone who's not?*

At the same time, I was very involved in the black church, which had a kind of a normalizing effect to what was happening in society. I think that is a very purposeful evangelical move in black communities to gain allies for conservative causes. And so I was conflicted there.

My response was, *Well, I need to be an even better citizen. I need to do all of the things that society tells me I need to do in order to effect change—finish college, go to law school, become a lawyer.*

I entered Brooklyn Law School in 1998. I had never been in a white space before. In February of 1999, an unarmed twenty-three-year-old Guinean named Amadou Diallo was shot to death by the NYPD. They fired forty-one shots!

The challenge for me was: were these cops going to be prosecuted? Was there going to be a substantial change in policies, practices and procedures? And when I went to the law school, it was almost like you couldn't really bring it up in a conversation; people would change the subject. It was treated as an anomaly. Like, "Yeah, this thing happened, but it happened in a vacuum and that doesn't really happen."

But from my experience, it happened all the time. It just wasn't publicized. And this one was publicized. So I felt enraged, like no one's paying attention to this black man who was gunned down in the vestibule of his apartment by the police, and no one's accountable.

So I came to school in a white T-shirt that had bullet holes in it and had red writing, "41 shots." Admittedly, it may have been a performative gesture. But it was what I did. I felt compelled to at least let people know that I was uncomfortable, and if you were going to be around me then you were going to be uncomfortable until we had a conversation about what happened. It showed me just how much of society, particularly white society, is trying not to see what's happening across the other side, and that was disheartening for me. Still, that wasn't my moment.

While not practicing law, I relied on income from consulting on music and film projects and I produced two albums: C3's gospel, "Release Me" and Ro James's R&B, "Eldorado." At the same time, I went back and studied the life of Fred Hampton, in terms of how he organized, in terms of how he communicated with people on different levels, not just based on race, not just based on class, not just based on political or social or economic philosophies, but on a very practical level.

I restudied the life of Malcolm X. Martin Luther King after he came out against the Vietnam War. Kwame Ture. Bayard Rustin. I was looking at all of these people and saying, "Wow, there's a real spectrum of social and political thought that I've never really tapped into, that can really help me as a human being and help me as an advocate."

I thought, *Okay, I'm back as a lawyer. And I'm going to do this*. One of my first clients was a black woman who accused a high-profile lawyer of raping her. From that case, police brutality cases came my way; wrongful arrest cases came, as did Title Seven employment discrimination cases. I mean, these things just started to come immediately because I made space for them. Saying, "This is what I'm going to do."

Typically you want prestige, you want to be up above the street in an office, away from people. But my law partner Kenneth Montgomery and I said, "No, we're going to have a high-level litigation practice in a storefront in a middle class neighborhood where it's very visible, where we're very approachable."

In 2013, while still practicing law, I joined a group of friends—lawyers, designers, people in the agency space—to form the Brooklyn

Combine. Most of us are from either Brownsville, Crown Heights, parts of Brooklyn, and two of the guys are from Newark. We have all different skill sets, but we have a common value system to make sure that our communities are in charge of their narratives.

Our collective grew out of something we noticed when we visited our clients in jails: that the jails feel like the public schools in terms of the architecture, in terms of the spacing, cages, staircases, how the food is served. I mean, it's a replica of the prison system. So, what we did is, we said, "We're going to attack that."

We started going into schools on Wednesday evenings and Saturdays and providing mentoring, discussing with kids what they want to do, what their goals are, what they're passionate about. And we align them with people who work in the field, who can kind of provide them with a North Star for where they want to go.

The second thing that we do is teach STEAM and STEM focus coding so that kids are not just speaking the language that's given to them, but they're learning how to write that language. They're learning how to design video games. They're learning how intentional some of the programming is in the things that they watch and enjoy.

And so once we start opening them up to how intentional some of the things are, then they become curious about other things. And then that opens us up to the third thing, which is a critical analysis, critical thinking workshop. And that curriculum is something that we uniquely built. So we would bring in history lessons.

We will go through these critical analysis exercises, where we break down information that's given to us as a society, and we discuss why it's being given to us, what it means to us, how it affects us, and what are some of our potential responses to the information. That was revolutionary because now the kids were going back home and having conversations with their parents. And their parents' response was: "Oh, I want to come in and sit in a meeting."

So our Saturday program started out as a program for middle school–aged kids, and it grew and turned into an all-ages program where we had a few grandmothers. We had people as old as seventy-nine. And kids as young as seven and eight. All in a circle learning together.

We try to impress upon kids that the most important thing you need to focus on is being responsible to your community. And if you anchor or you center being responsible to your community, then "the protest" is actually one of the mechanisms. It's not the only mechanism. It's not something where you say, "Oh, we disagree with this, so we'll protest." If it's irresponsible to protest and it doesn't actually get you to the goal, then it doesn't matter.

We want to make sure that we're not embracing the value systems that we're protesting. What I mean by that is, sometimes we can say, "Oh, I don't like something and so. . ." For example, this whole cancel culture thing that's happening now.

Cancel culture is a tool of the oppressor. American society has canceled history, right? We re-envision history so that we pretend indigenous people never existed, we pretend slavery never existed, we pretend Japanese internment didn't exist, we pretend we're not the only country that dropped nuclear bombs on other places. The idea of canceling someone or canceling a history of the existence of something is an American thing.

The practice of canceling is actually just embracing the oppressor's value system as opposed to saying, "No, we're rejecting this oppressive value system wholesale. We're going to, instead of cancel stuff, we're going to confront it. We're going to call it out, we're going to challenge it, and we're going to engage in this hard work that it takes to actually become who we need to be collectively." Because we're all on this planet. And we can't pretend a cross section of us doesn't exist. That just doesn't work.

To people who lament that they are too busy with work to become involved in collective engagement, I'd recommend they find ways to make their passion intersect with their profession. I've been able to use skills as a nonprofit leader that transfer and apply to my work as an attorney and advocate. My passion for advocacy informs my ability to develop strong skills in the courtroom as well as in the boardroom of nonprofits.

And to those who may have suffered setbacks and found the need to reexamine their values, I'd advise: never spend time trying to convince people that you are good, just be good. Never chase what you want in life, just be what you desire and you'll attract everything that you need. And remember the words of Bayard Rustin: "We need in every society, a group of angelic troublemakers."

FOR MORE INFORMATION:
www.bklyncombine.com
www.keithwhitelaw.com

'If We Don't Teach the Truth'

MELISSA "MISSY" JANCZEWSKI JONES, *51, is a historian whose focus is African American history during the Reconstruction era and historical memory. A former paralegal, she is currently director of Paralegal Studies and Public History in the Department of History and Political Science at Mississippi College in Clinton, Mississippi. She received her bachelor's and master's degrees from that school and is a PhD candidate in American history at the University of Southern Mississippi.*

GEORGE COUNTY, WHERE I grew up in south Mississippi, is 90 percent white, and about 10 percent African American. There's a big disparity there in terms of population. But because my mother taught at a school that had a mix of black and white students, I went to that school instead of the one closer to our home that was almost all white.

My best friend from day one in kindergarten was an African American girl named Sheila. We wanted so much to go to each other's homes and to play, but my family would not allow me to go to her house. And, of course, they wouldn't allow her to come with me to my house and play. I think that was the moment that I began to realize: *This just doesn't feel right. This is Sheila, this is my friend. What are you trying to tell me? I just know her as my friend, and she's my friend, no matter what.* So those two things didn't make sense to me.

I was brought up to specifically see color and to think of people in terms of color and in terms of a sense of hierarchy. But I was also brought up in a family that was very religious. From a very early age, those two incongruent things just never made sense to me.

Both of my parents were born in 1944. They met in college in Mississippi. They were from different places—my dad came from Rome, New York, and my mom was from this neck of the woods—but they roughly held the same beliefs. Between the two of them, my dad was the more racist; he used the N-word his whole life. My mom just had those ingrained beliefs from growing up in a very rural part of Mississippi.

It was very difficult to ask my parents questions about race. There weren't a lot of opportunities for activism growing up. If anything, my protest was subtle and silent; it was in the friends that I made and kept. It didn't matter to me—gay, straight, black, white, you name it. And that was a difficult time with regard to race and sexual identity in that part of Mississippi. I wasn't very vocal. It was more of a private, relational use of my sense of empathy, more than my voice.

When I turned eighteen, I just wanted live somewhere else—which I've done. I went off to college. I met my husband there, and after graduation, we moved to Fort Worth, Texas, where he went to seminary. I worked in a law office for eight years before we came back to Mississippi in 2000, and I continued to telecommute for that firm for the next decade.

We'd had our two children by 2000 and made a conscious decision to come back to Mississippi to raise them here. We both felt we had left things unfinished with regard to race and wanted to make a difference. For my husband, that was in nonprofit work and then ultimately as a pastor in a church. For me, it was raising our children and continuing to work remotely. Then I decided I wanted to know more about African American history, particularly Reconstruction, so I went back to school.

After beginning my master's work, I became curious about a historical marker in Clinton. The pole was standing, but there was no plaque. A fellow church member, Ricky Nations, told me the marker had gone missing in the late 1980s and that it had noted several historical events, including the "Clinton Riot of 1875." I'd never heard of that and neither had a lot of other people.

Jones has devoted her master's and PhD work to chronicling the true story of the event and to commemorating it with a plaque. In 2015, thanks in large part to Jones, the city's historical committee unveiled a new marker, albeit at a different and less visible site than originally intended. It reads:

On September 4, 1875, Charles Caldwell, a former slave and Republican state senator, organized a rally at "Moss Hill." Firing erupted during the rally attended by more than 1500 blacks and about 75 whites, including some white Democrats. During the ensuing melee at least four whites and five blacks were killed but in the next few days many more blacks were killed by vigilante mobs from nearby towns. The violence served as a pretext for the return of white rule and the end of Reconstruction in Mississippi.

While the 2015 marker still references the inaccurate and outdated term of the "Clinton Riot," Jones observes that it was the first historical marker to ever acknowledge white-on-black violence in the state of Mississippi. She also notes that a newer and more visible marker was installed in Clinton as a part of the Mississippi Freedom Trail in 2021 and refers to the Clinton Massacre, not "Riot."

Throughout Reconstruction, and in other traumatic time periods, there were similar racial massacres. A lot of what was done was covered up or blamed on African Americans, and this is reflected in the primary sources I've read. That's what happened in Clinton. A lot of the violence was blamed on the black community. But that was not the case. This was a premeditated event committed by [then] white Democrats to regain political control. They used the specter of a black uprising or a black insurrection that would have existed in the minds of whites to plot this sort of insurrection and mass violence.

The black vote was significantly suppressed thanks to the terror committed by these white terrorists. In 1875, the Democrats, who had lost by thirty thousand votes in the previous election two years earlier, won by thirty thousand votes and took back control of Mississippi, basically ending the Republican policies of Reconstruction.

While working on my master's degree, I had a professor who said, "Don't just write about that event; think about why it matters." He taught History and Memory classes, which got me thinking, *Okay, how has the story been told in historical writings and also in public history and in the classroom? Or more importantly, how and why has it not been told or been mis-told?*

That's why researching the Clinton Massacre is so important—because it shows that critical divide. And that's why my dissertation is titled: "The Clinton Massacre of 1875: Dueling Histories and Reconstruction Memory in the Deep South."

It matters what we teach and how we teach it, and what the truth is. If we don't teach the truth about the past, we can never really hope to create a better world going forward or deal with the trauma of the past. There was so much racial trauma and hurt done in this community, and that has so many ripple effects. The more people that I talk to in the local black community, the more I realize that this is still true. I don't think a lot of people in Clinton today realize the depth of the hurt and the trauma that an event that happened almost one hundred fifty years ago actually caused and the necessity to actually come to terms with that. It's not just rehashing the past, as some might say. It's actually bringing into the light of day what was never dealt with at the time and what was mis-taught and mis-told in Mississippi for so long.

After the white Democrats regained control in Mississippi in 1875, the U.S. Senate sent a committee to Mississippi led by Senator George Boutwell of Massachusetts to look into why there were such voting irregularities. The result was a two thousand-page volume called the "Boutwell Report," which has been available, but buried for years. It's been a major source for my research because it includes a lot of people's personal testimonies.

I've also interviewed people of color here in Clinton for my dissertation. There are many who have ancestors connected to the massacre. I've tried to work slowly and with a lot of integrity. I don't want to ever come across as exploiting those relationships. I want to be seen as someone who's going to walk with them through this journey and not someone who's just coming in to do an interview, to take what I want.

Unfortunately, the marker the city put up in 2015 has been knocked down twice and isn't up currently. I'm glad the 2021 marker, which was created by the local African American churches, is in a safer place. Visibility is absolutely important for any marker telling public history. This one is closer to the spot where the massacre took place, which is also important. I hope the other one gets put back up and in a more protected spot.

One of the things that I found in my research was that when the 1949 marker was removed, nothing was ever put in its place until 2015, and you had this gap in historical memory. A certain generation, like my friend Ricky Nations and others, had been reminded of that event when they passed that marker but during that almost thirty-plus years gap, when there was no marker, it was really easy for the city to just allow it to be forgotten. That allowed a whole generation of people moving into Clinton or people being born and then growing up in Clinton to not know about it or be reminded about it at all.

In teaching African American history and elements of public history, one is an activist by nature. I think for me it's being consciously aware of inequalities and being empathetic and sensitive to those inequalities and doing everything in my power, to the extent that I have power, to right them—whether it's by educating young men and women to be more empathetic, or providing the best education possible regardless of someone's ethnicity, or providing jobs when I'm in a hiring capacity.

What motivates me most are my personal relationships. So my advice is seek out those relationships with people that don't look like you, that might not identify the same way that you do, that might not believe the same way that you do, and just listen; just absolutely be quiet and listen. Don't go in with any idea of changing anyone's mind, but instead say, "I just wanna hear your experience. I wanna know what your perception of things are." If we have more people willing to engage in those kind of relationships and conversations, the rest of it will come out of that. It's all about empathy.

It's okay to be vulnerable, but if you want someone to be vulnerable with you, you have to be willing to be vulnerable. That's such an honored, sacred space that when someone gives you that, you really have to treasure it.

FOR MORE INFORMATION:
https://www.mc.edu/faculty/u/jones20
https://www.mshistorynow.mdah.ms.gov/issue/the
-clinton-riot-of-1875-from-riot-to-massacre

'By Raising Awareness'

KAHLIL GREENE, 22, *a recent graduate of Yale, was that school's first black student body president. He is a self-described "Gen-Z Inclusion Expert," with over fifteen million views on TikTok. He has been featured in the* New York Times, *and his op-eds have appeared in such publications as the* Washington Post *and* Harvard Business Review.

I GREW UP IN Montgomery County, Maryland. I went to majority black and Latinx elementary and middle schools. But for high school, I went to an elite magnet program in Poolesville, a very white town on the wealthier side of the county. It's a place where there were large white supremacist rallies in the 1950s. Very rural. Very conservative. I was the only black student in a class of sixty students. The rest were East Asian or South Asian or white.

When I was in this program, I experienced racism upfront. The kids would make jokes about me being the only black person. They said really mean, racist things; the N word was thrown around a lot. They would say all this with a laugh, as if they were joking. It wasn't said with the same sort of vitriol and actual violence that would be directed at someone in the 1960s. Their attitude was more like, *it's over now. Like people aren't really racist. Like we can say these things as a joke to you. And it'll be funny.* But it was racist still. And it still hurt. That was what I experienced on the personal level. At the larger level, I was always questioning why there were no other black kids in this program.

My parents would tell me to just keep my head down, to just get through. But I didn't just sit there and take it. I called the students taunting me names back, which in this age of social media is not necessarily the ideal thing to do. It did get me into trouble sometimes, which is scary to think about given the dynamic of the school-to-prison pipeline for young black men. Often the person retaliating is the one who gets caught and gets into trouble.

I think an activist is someone who identifies issues within society and works specifically to target and solve those issues—especially if they're centered around inequality or injustice. My activism comes mainly from experiences in my own life. My parents definitely raised me with a level of social consciousness around injustice, especially related to their experiences as black people born in the 1960s and raised in America. But though I had a knowledge of these issues growing up, I wouldn't say I necessarily had a desire or drive or opportunity to really address them until high school.

A lot of what we learn about injustice revolves around blacks and whites; the suggestion is it's binary. But the dynamic can be more complex. As I said, there were a lot of Asian American students within this program at the school. They would say things to the effect that they were minorities, too, nonwhite. Then they'd say, like, "Asians are successful, so why can't black people be successful."

This is the "model minority" myth. That sentiment was something that dominated my entire high school experience and something I only really started to interrogate towards the end of my time in high school. I wrote my college essays about that, and that's what helped me to get into to Yale.

Once I got into Yale, I found an environment where it wasn't just about getting into college and doing really well in terms of STEM courses and the other things that the magnet was focused on. I was able to develop ideas that were related to a variety of new disciplines—History, Sociology, Political Science. It was an environment where those academic subjects were a part of discussions at all times. So it was in college where I was able to start making actual change toward those injustice issues that I faced or observed.

I got involved in student government my freshman year, and as a sophomore, I became the Finance Director of the Yale College Council. In this role, I worked on funding important projects like getting free menstrual hygiene products put in every residential college. Then I ran for student body president and was the first black person ever elected to that position at Yale.

Four days after my election, there was the shooting of an unarmed black woman at the hands of the Yale Police Department. That led to my first time having to help coordinate and organize a protest alongside New Haven activists. And it was my first real moment on the streets in front of police officers.

What people may not realize is that a lot of what happens for a protest to succeed is logistics. I gave one short speech with a megaphone during the protest, but the real work happened earlier in the day: I had my laptop and my phone and I worked with the head of the Afro-American cultural center and another activist, following them around, typing out messages, coordinating the flyers, making sure everyone knew what the issues were, where the protests were taking place and how they could help. My recognition from being featured in the *Yale Daily News* as recently elected, and, I think, being the school's first student body president involved in this kind of protest lent itself to other students feeling more empowered.

When the pandemic came, we students went home. After the George Floyd murder, there were marches in Montgomery County. They were fine, but they didn't seem that effective in addressing the issue because a lot of those protesting sought to march side by side with local police. So I asked myself: *What can I do to actually help people from my living room?*

I organized a fundraiser, which ended up raising fifty-seven thousand dollars in one week. To advertise that, I had to write an op-ed, my first for the *Yale Daily News*. I did a lot of research. I like writing. Good writing has a smooth flow like good poetry or rap.

The piece was about George Floyd, Ahmaud Arbery, and Breonna Taylor, and what police brutality means to the Yale community. It read in part:

> For Black people in America, racial violence can take our lives anywhere and at any time. It doesn't matter if we think we are safe. It doesn't matter if we are "good people." It doesn't even matter how educated we are. Black is still Black, even in Yale Blue.

The money went to initiatives tackling the effects of racism in the black community and to support the health crisis in the Navajo Nation.

A few weeks after the op-ed, I made an Instagram infographic about the holiday, Juneteenth. It went viral. I really like the process of writing and using graphics to get my message across. This has led to a social media presence where I have over five hundred thousand followers and twenty million-plus views across the TikTok, Instagram, and LinkedIn platforms. This is the best outlet for my activism, as are more op-eds in places like the *Washington Post*. I always try to find a new slant on what I'm writing about.

Having recently graduated, I'm doing full-time social media work, a lot of which overlaps with topics that I care about—the 2021 Capitol riots, the 1898 Wilmington Massacre. I consider myself an online educator even though not all my work is on these subjects; some is funded by writing about brands.

There's a really good book called *You Are More Powerful Than You Think* by Eric Liu. He talks about two concepts—and I wrote an op-ed about this too—"Reading Power and Writing Power." To read power is to understand how institutions and social groups are set up and understand how they exercise political influence to make a change or keep the status quo. To write power is to implement and execute the strategies necessary to change policy and enact reform. To read power is to learn. To write power is to act.

In my case, I really like to read in depth and then write. For example, in eventually researching that Model Minority myth at my high school, I learned that when the civil rights movement ended, Congress passed immigration acts that mostly allowed professionals from Asia to come to the United States. So a lot of the kids around me in the magnet program were from the most educated and wealthiest families. Their history here is nothing like the history of black Americans, brought here against their will in forced slavery and then subjected to Jim Crow laws. All those things are very different; even though we're both people of color, we're very different in terms of our heritage and our historical experiences, and that results in these disparities between races.

Being able to articulate that is something I can do now, but I definitely would not have been able to wrap my head around that when I was in high school. Once you have this understanding, that's when you start reading even more to find out what solutions exist. And you follow that by raising awareness. Understanding on your own is always the first step. Then you just tell people about it and come up with ideas and solutions.

Learning how to be a persuasive advocate with your written and spoken word is really important. I think a lot of the changemakers that we have had throughout history—whether it be the Martin Luther King, Jr., Malcolm Xs or whoever you want to think about—they have all been really great orators, as well as people who could write a speech very clearly with metaphors and repetition and the conviction in their voices to persuade people to see the world from their side. Those speeches are riveting even to this day. And I think that's because those leaders were great at persuading people to make things better. That's what I'm trying to do.

FOR MORE INFORMATION:
  kahlilgreene.com
  www.tiktok.com/@kahlilgreene
  www.instagram.com/kahlil.greene/

'Fostering Greater Civic Participation'

CLARISSA MARTINEZ DE CASTRO, *55, is deputy vice president for Policy and Advocacy at Washington, D.C.-based UnidosUS (formerly National Council of La Raza), the nation's largest Latino civil rights and advocacy organization. There she leads efforts to advance fair and effective immigration policies and to expand Latino civic engagement by helping immigrants become citizens, citizens become voters, and the community overall become an active participant in policy debates. Martinez De Castro holds a master's degree from Harvard's Kennedy School of Government and a bachelor's degree from Occidental College. She became a naturalized U.S citizen in 2001.*

DEPENDING ON HOW YOU look at it, you could say I am an accidental advocate for social justice, or, that it was fate I be one. Either way, it was not the result of some plan I laid out or of a specific moment, but rather of life experiences shaped by a series of fortunate—and sometimes unfortunate—events.

I was born and raised in Mexico, one of seven kids. My mom was a homemaker and a seamstress. My dad had a little record store. They didn't have the chance to go to college, but wanted that for us. I remember them reading the paper every day and talking about what was happening around us.

My parents weren't activists in the conventional sense, but I remember my mother getting incensed when she heard about people being taken advantage of—whether it was by a neighbor or a corrupt politician—and lending a hand where she could. That's why I define activism as putting care, and hope, into action. It doesn't have to be a world-changing act; it's also about the things we do in our daily life. It's important to demystify what people may think activism and advocacy are and to see that we all are able to do it. Because it is the aggregate of all those actions that can bring about change.

Like eleven million people in our country today, I was an un-documented immigrant. And like those today, I found myself here because of the ideal of America. I cannot take credit for the courage it took to leave the familiar, break with tradition and venture into the unknown. That credit goes to my mother. I just followed, kicking and screaming. I was a teenager then. Suddenly my world changed. I didn't speak English or know how things worked. I was so afraid of that first school day, I thought about breaking my leg to avoid it. But I did what had to be done. Just like my mother did. She was prob-ably afraid, too. But she had no time to wallow. She had problems to solve. And that is something we can all relate to, even if the situation we face is different.

As a seamstress, my mom took whatever jobs she could. My first job was in the garment district, too. It gave me a real appreciation for how long and hard she and so many others work and yet, because of the nature of those jobs, can barely keep their head above water. There's this false perception constantly pushed on us that if people don't do well or are poor, it's because something is wrong with them. But when you live it, you know it's just that: false. Imagine if all the energy people are forced to spend just to survive could be unleashed to thrive, as those who have more opportunity do. We should be working to achieve that, and it would benefit us all.

As my English got better, I often had to help my family translate and navigate situations, as many children of immigrants do. It's a dif-ferent role than a regular teenager would have. It makes you see the struggles people have when we are not able to understand each other, and how things that should be simple become incredibly difficult. I was becoming a translator, literally and figuratively, helping make sense of the world around us.

Imagine, through all that uncertainty and the fear you may be separated, how tightly family pulls together to make it through. Imagine teachers, counselors and others along the way who could have stood by, but instead helped you "make it." Though I couldn't put it into words then, I was learning the meaning of "I am my brother's keeper." Sure, I worked hard. But let's not kid ourselves. I'm indebted to the strength of family, the kindness of strangers—and a lot of luck. Many have not been so lucky. And the thing is, luck should not be the determining factor in how people fare.

Speaking of luck—when I started tenth grade at Garfield High in East LA, my frame of reference was from American movies. The ones I'd seen showed kids in locker rooms, half-dressed or naked. Let's just say I was not used to that. Looking for an alternative, I got signed up for Junior ROTC. I had no idea what that was, but it was not PE. What it turned out to be was two of the many kind strangers along my way. Realizing they had several kids like me who were English learners, the two retired sergeants that ran the program tutored us before and after school. And sergeants as they were, they pushed me. After a time they said, "Look, we know you can, but are reluctant to speak it. So we're only going to respond to you if you speak to us in English." They were not being mean; at that point they knew I could do it, but was embarrassed and they helped push through that. I think that's one of the reasons I started getting better faster.

Over the next two years, Martinez De Castro excelled in high school. A guidance counselor willing to go the extra mile helped her overcome her reluctance to fill out college applications because she was undocumented and even contacted schools on her behalf. She was admitted to Occidental College and initially considered majoring in Microbiology. But even after surviving Organic Chemistry, she decided to switch and graduated with a degree in Diplomacy and World Affairs.

As graduation approached, she was uncertain of what she was going to do. Then the director of the Upward Bound program where she was working suggested she apply for a job with a labor union. She had never considered working for organized labor, but interviewed and went on to work for two unions, both of which represented workers like her mother—in the restaurant, hotel, and garment industries.

After a couple of years with the unions, she was approached by a former professor and took a job at the University of Southern California on a project bringing together leaders from California and Mexico to build a shared understanding on issues facing both regions. From there she went to an organization working with a handful of others to include a bi-national development bank and worker and environmental protections in the North American Free Trade Agreement (NAFTA). She'd never lobbied before, and only half-jokingly says the organization probably could not afford someone with more experience. The effort achieved some significant victories, and she is thankful for experiencing that, since it is not always the case and legislative efforts often take years to come to fruition if at all.

Mine has not been a linear path. Particularly early on, some of it had to do with not knowing what to look for or how, not having close family who had walked those paths, or not having networks. But some of it also has to do with saying, "Okay, I'll try that," when necessity required it or when interesting things came along, both of which involved overcoming the fear of venturing into something new or unknown to me. Much like stepping into that high school campus many years back.

Despite being a nonlinear path, there are common threads. Whether we were trying to improve conditions in a particular sewing shop; create a better understanding between leaders in the U.S. and Mexico; or trying to get legislators to create a bank and worker and environmental protections; or the work I do today, there have always been elements of translation and change. Translation, in navigating different perspectives and situations to help demystify and make sense of things, as I did for my family early on, and now applying that in other arenas.

I think being an advocate is very much about translating, about creating meaning and helping people understand or relate to experiences and perspectives that are different from their own. As for change, well, whether it was my family's journey seeking opportunity, or learning from those experiences to put in my own *granito de arena* to try to improve conditions for people facing similar challenges, or figuring out different ways of doing depending the job I was able to have, change has been a constant.

Through the NAFTA effort, I had a chance to work with and later get hired by Charles Kamasaki, who was then Vice President of Policy at National Council of La Raza [now UnidosUS] and one of the advocates who years back made possible the legislation that allowed me to legalize my status and eventually become a United States citizen. I've been at the organization a shocking, by today's standards, twenty-six years.

I know this sounds contradictory for someone who talks about change as a constant. But while here I've had a chance to do very different things in a variety of places—from immigration policy in D.C., to workforce development and health advocacy in Texas, to education and access for DREAMers in California, to polling and electoral participation in multiple states, and other things in between. I eventually returned to D.C. to create a project focused on increasing civic participation, something near and dear to my heart.

I believe that a strong civil society is a necessary ingredient for solving many of the challenges we are facing. And there are so many forces at play trying to undermine the voice of our civil society, and fueling fear and distrust to extinguish our ability to come together to solve problems. So for me, working on fostering greater civic participation is a way to contribute, in whatever modest way, to a stronger civil society. My present job working with the Latino community is about building a continuum: helping eligible immigrants become citizens; then helping citizens, whether naturalized or native born, become voters; and helping the community regardless of status or age to become more vocal in the issues that impact them and their families. Because you don't need to have a particular status or be eighteen or older to make a difference. There are many ways to participate.

As for voting: every election cycle I hear some of the same old, tired and incorrect statements about the Latino community, calling us "a sleeping giant" or "apathetic." Something is getting lost in translation—a good example of why cultural competence, real understanding, matters. A community that works this hard, that has a higher labor participation rate than any other group, that believes in family and country, is not "apathetic." It's "unconvinced."

Many are tired of being neglected, or worse, demonized, and wonder if their participation will really make a difference in creating change. So they decide to focus their energy on the things that they feel they have more power over and will directly impact their families. Many others are not familiar with the process as is, let alone with the increasing number of obstacles being created to prevent people from voting. We have seen that when you engage in conversation with people, when you help navigate and demystify the process, and invite them in, the majority will participate. What you often hear is that nobody had ever bothered to talk to them about it.

In either case, what I've learned along the way is that it is when things seem harder and more intractable, when circumstances may make us want to disengage and throw in the towel, that's when we need to show up the most. And because our country's diversity is one of our greatest national assets—helping us navigate a complex world, innovate and problem-solve—it is critical to have a strong civil society, and accountable elected leaders, who reflect our myriad lived experiences, challenges and shared aspirations.

That's how we help ourselves avoid making wrong assumptions

about people in whose shoes we have not walked, better understand the cause and effect of how different systems are impacting people's ability to thrive, and what we can do together to change it. That, in ways big and small, is what being an advocate for social justice means to me.

FOR MORE INFORMATION:
   www.unidosus.org
   www.becomeavoter.org

'Building a Multi-racial Working Class Coalition'

JULIAN D. MILLER, *36, is a Mississippi-based lawyer, law professor, and community organizer who cofounded the Reuben V. Anderson Center for Justice to address systemic poverty through programs in the areas of economic justice, public health equity, educational equity and criminal justice equity. He has also worked in creating sustainable community food systems.*

WHEN I WAS GROWING up in the 1990s, my uncle was the mayor of my hometown Winstonville, Mississippi, population of about three hundred. At the time, he was the longest serving African-American mayor in the United States. Winstonville is in the heart of the Mississippi Delta, which is the second poorest region in America. He got us the first post office, first voting precinct, and first police and fire vehicles. He built a city hall and established a homeless shelter and low-income housing units. That was an inspiration for me in thinking about what I wanted to do as a career and leveraging that work into systemic policy change—developing those type of resources and job and business opportunities to create wealth in low-income communities. Seeing that laid the foundation for my activism, which was more solidified once I got to college and started community organizing work.

I'm a fifth generation Mississippi Deltan. My mother was my hero. She was a chemist and community college professor who decided to fulfill her lifelong dream of becoming a doctor. She enrolled in medical school when I was seven and became an obstetrician-gynecologist and family medicine doctor. Later, she worked in American Samoa in the National Health Service Corps and started a rural health clinic.

We were very close, and she thought I'd go into medicine, too. I liked the idea. There's nothing more noble you can do than keep someone from dying when they don't have to, right? I was a human being, I had morals, I was a Christian. So I wanted to do some good to make the world better off.

I pivoted when I was in high school. Being a doctor, saving a life, was a worthwhile endeavor. But I thought I could do more if I were in politics, because it touched every issue: healthcare, education, economics, the whole nine yards. The people around me were poor and powerless economically. And don't get me started on how bad the school system was. I thought it would be much more gratifying to do something where I could give a person a life worth living and address all of these areas through public policy and service.

I went to Harvard for college, majored in Government, and graduated in 2007. The sky's the limit there. I literally believed I could do anything I put my mind to. For a while I thought I might be a screenwriter. And when thinking about politics, I thought I might end up in Washington. But then after my sophomore year, my grandmother got sick. She had basically raised me while my mother went back to school. So I took a leave of absence and went back home to help take care of her.

That summer of 2005 I worked at the Kemetic Institute, a not-for-profit in Mound Bayou that offers mentoring, tutoring, and teaches civic engagement, which I also did in the Boston schools at Harvard.

While home that year, I got some amazing opportunities. After Hurricane Katrina, I got the chance to work with my uncle. As an officer of the National Conference of Black Mayors, he was tasked with providing direct services to people coming from New Orleans who were in need. I helped him set up the Community Relief Foundation. Then I served as Policy Director for the 2006 congressional campaign of Chuck Espy, which gave me some understanding of how you link policy to actually improving the material lot of people's lives.

Ironically enough, by the time I graduated, I was thinking maybe politics is not the most effective means by which to facilitate the type of change to the system that's necessary. The reality was this system effectively neutralized the type of collective organizing of poor and working-class people that would be necessary to move economic policy to the left, where the country could be more of a social democracy characterized by universal economic rights in health care, education, and living-wage job security and where people again could have greater material benefits in their lives and actually reap more of the benefits of their labor. I realized I needed to get engaged in more grassroots organizing and in helping build capacity of the work being done on the ground in order to lay the groundwork for substantive policy change.

It was very motivating for me to come back home. I think activism has to begin with what's important to you at some level in your own life. People have all of these ideals and all these aspirations, and it's great. But if you can't help the folks that are right around you—-family, friends, people in your community—I mean, it's difficult to be able to help those people or issues that you share no intimate connection with. There's something to be said for first making your own house a home before you move on to someone else's. People who come here—often called "outsiders"—who don't understand the problems of those communities and don't do a good job of engaging the people are going to have a hard time being effective.

Starting in the spring of 2008, I spent three years as a Program Coordinator for the Dreyfus Health Foundation, which had started anti-poverty work in the Delta about five years earlier. We worked with academic institutions, hospitals, clinics, government agencies and other community organizations to create better health and economic opportunities.

During this time, I reconnected with my first grade teacher, Sister Theresa. She was working with a group of girls from middle school and high school to create a community service project they called Clutter2Compost. The idea was to collect yard waste that under a new law couldn't be burned, break it down, turn it into compost, and then sell bags of compost. I helped them write a grant for this project, which they received.

Clutter2Compost was a self-sustaining project that addressed an environmental issue in their community while having the potential to be a sustainable enterprise. This experience made me realize that economic justice would have to be essential to my anti-poverty work. I started thinking about how we could create worker-owned economies from homegrown industry in the Mississippi Delta that could provide people living wages while at the same time create revenue to address the systemic, social problems in this region to achieve better schools, health care, and social services. That led to the idea of developing a sustainable community food system.

Some pioneering work had already been done on that front. The Delta has some of the most fertile soil in the country. It also has large farms owned by whites who are more committed to cash crops like cotton and corn. Years ago—not by accident—these farms replaced most of the black-owned farms, and people of color were now working on them for almost slave wages. But beginning in the 1990s, a group of African American farmers in the Delta formed an organization called Mississippians Engaging in Greener Agriculture (MEGA) and had expanded their use of small plots of land and other innovative methods to grow fresh local produce and take the food to farmers' markets.

My thought was to organize, build capacity, develop these collective food systems, and then capture revenue to support all those social and economic services I previously mentioned. So in 2010, we started the Delta Fresh Foods Initiative (DFFI), which included growers, consumers, health and agriculture educators, food retailers including farmers' markets and other outlets, community-based organizations, funders, healthy food advocates and more.

DFFI was able to develop over sixty community garden projects throughout the Mississippi Delta. We started a mobile market and sold produce to individual consumers at markets and eventually started selling to a local hotel. We built a six-acre youth farm in order to have more stable production to support our mobile market and scale our enterprise to serve the greater Mississippi Delta community.

We have a woman who does produce canning and things like that. So we're building up other producers. We've had youth ambassadors who've created brochures and gone to churches to explain the importance of healthy eating. We had a cooking class component. The ultimate goal is for the local communities to take ownership of this initiative and make it sustainable.

In 2011, I left Dreyfus for law school and then for private practice and a position as an adjunct professor at Mississippi College of Law in Jackson. But I continue to organize. I've remained involved with DFFI, and a fellow lawyer Raina Anderson and I have established the Reuben V. Anderson Center for Justice in partnership with Tougaloo College and other institutions.

Our mission is to address systemic poverty through programs in four areas: economic justice, public health equity, educational equity and criminal justice equity. For example, as part of our educational equity project, we provide mentoring and academic enrichment support to middle school students in Jackson public schools led by college students. Additionally, we established an urban model for community food system development and built a farm and food system at historic Tougaloo College, a prestigious HBCU with a strong legacy of civil rights activism and social justice. I currently serve on the faculty of Tougaloo doing this work.

It's important to inspire young people to be proactive about these issues—to read, get educated and get these opportunities. God bless those who want to become involved. But those of us already engaged in the work have to be deliberate about presenting them strategic ways to address the issues they think are important.

For young people who are passionate and motivated, it is important to look at who's doing this work in your community. Look at who's already involved. Also look for advice and mentoring. If you're a young person, you can have the inspiration, have the ideas, know what you want to do, read about it, but the next step is you want to get it done. In other words, you need wisdom—which is knowing how to do what to do. You can only get that through mentorship.

Collective action means what it says: *collective*. If you want to engage and address an issue and organize around it, identify who is like-minded. Whether another young person, older person, or organization is already engaged, I promise you, we need more bodies. We need more people supporting this work.

From my perspective, I understand this is going to be a marathon, not a sprint. It took hundreds of years for the Delta to become this way. So change is not going to happen in six months. The idea is building a multi-racial working class coalition, to keep advancing and moving the ball in the right direction. To give you an example of what we have now that we didn't have when I started: we have something called the Mississippi Food Justice Collaborative, which is a statewide coalition of activists, organizers, farmers, and growers who are actually trying to develop a statewide community food system to address both economic injustice and public health inequity in the state.

What makes someone an activist is taking the actual time and effort—whether it be through protest, civil disobedience, running for political office, joining organizations, or working in the nonprofit sector—to address those issues that have affected their lives and the lives of others.

Those who are engaging in activism believe that, despite this unjust political and economic system that ultimately caters to the wealthy interests of the country, through our own actions and by collectively working with others we can advance the ball and materially improve the lives of the majority of working people and poor people in this country.

I started this work when I was twenty-three and I'm thirty-six, thirteen years in. I'm still pushing, still inspired. And we're better off than we once were in this work. I have accepted the fact that I'm going to keep pushing as long as God puts breath in my body. But I'm comfortable that whenever I leave here, I will have laid the foundation for it to continue to advance. I'm still motivated, inspired, and I hope others can be as well.

FOR MORE INFORMATION:
    https://rvacenterforjustice.org
    https://www.tougaloo.edu/academics/divisions
        /social-science/pre-law/about-director

'Writing Was the Best Way'

BRANDY COLBERT, *43, is an award-winning author of several books for children with themes related to social justice. Her writing has been published in the* New York Times, *and her short stories and essays have appeared in several critically acclaimed anthologies for young people. She is on the faculty at Hamline University's MFA program in writing for children, and lives in Los Angeles.*

ABOUT FIFTEEN YEARS AGO, i started to become really interested in history. I came across an article that was commemorating the one hundredth anniversary of a triple lynching in my hometown, Springfield, Missouri. That just kind of blew my whole world up. I had never known about it, but it explained so much about why the town was so white-why it was only about 3 percent black when I was growing up in the 1980s and '90s.

It made me want to start digging deeper into a lot of stuff that I had never thought about before. At the same time I came across stories about activists I had never heard of, like Fannie Lou Hamer. That made me want to learn more, but also, as a writer, to make sure that others knew about these people who I didn't know about when I was younger and to try to help spread the word about events and people who had made such a big impact on black history.

My parents grew up in Jim Crow Arkansas at a time when everything was still segregated, you know, separate washrooms. They didn't talk much about it. Until I was older, I didn't really understand how hard their lives were and how different they were from the lives they gave me and my older brother.

My parents made sure that we were surrounded with positive black images. We went to a black church every Sunday, and my household had black magazines and books by black authors. I had black dolls. Barbie dolls! I don't even know how my parents found those in the 1980s. There was always a positive view of being black in our household, which I really appreciate, but I don't know if we really talked about it.

I had a nice middle class upbringing, never wanted for anything. My parents sent me to college. They made sure I was taken care of, but there was always this sense of survival when being out in the world, of knowing that you were being watched because you're different from everyone.

When I was sixteen, the hood of my car, which was parked in the employee lot of my job, was keyed with a racial slur. We never found out who did it. Traumatic events like that cause embarrassment and shame to anyone, but especially a sixteen-year-old. I felt like I had a lot of friends, but at the same time knew I was the "other" and that a lot of people didn't think I belonged where I lived.

I've been writing since I was about seven, and around that age, I started saying, "I want to be an author when I grow up." I knew it could be done, but I didn't know of many black authors who were publishing at that time, so it didn't seem like a viable career path. I started to really delve into the work of black authors in my late teens and college, but I still wasn't focused on writing about any kind of social justice issues. I just wanted to get published, and I wanted to write fiction.

I went to college in my hometown, at Missouri State University, and graduated with a degree in Journalism. There were newspapers and magazines in Springfield, but I felt there were people to see, places to go. Anyone I met in my hometown who was from a marginalized community, I was instantly drawn to because they knew what it was like to feel "othered." And so I imagined, *There must be many more people like us out in the world.*

So, less than a month after graduating from college, I moved to Los Angeles. About a year later, I got a job as an editorial assistant at a health and fitness magazine and began working my way up. Over the years, I kind of fell into the health and beauty beat, which I liked.

During this time, I started working to get published. I knew I wanted to write fiction, in particular Young Adult fiction. I wrote four books, and my fourth one, *Pointe*, was the first to get published. There are some conversations about race in there, but that's not the focus.

I began to write more directly about race in my novels after *Pointe*. My fifth novel and first middle grade book, *The Only Black Girls in Town*, deals with a lot of racial issues upfront, which was especially important to me, as I was writing for middle school readers. That was a turning point, where I thought, *I have something to say, and I know how to say it*. I could bring kids a story that I hoped was entertaining and fun and sweet, but also had some things that they might not know about at that age—like the concept of passing for white, or who was Emmett Till? Things that they might want to research on their own, or ask their parents about.

I started writing that book in 2018. I'm sure everything that was going on politically somehow made me think about how I could more effectively include social justice in my books going forward.

After that book, I was approached by an editor to write what became *The Voting Booth*. This whole book is, essentially, conveying a message, but I never want any of my writing to feel didactic, especially fiction. So it was sort of a tricky balance: trying to make the story fun, while also trying to insert some history about voting rights and the struggles still faced today when it comes to voting.

I went straight from that book to co-adapting an adult biography of Rosa Parks into a version for young adults. While I was working on that, I spoke with another editor about writing a book on the 1921 Tulsa Race Massacre. I was terrified, because even though I have a journalism degree and have worked in journalism for my entire adult life, I hadn't done this kind of long-form nonfiction project.

I wrote a proposal and it was accepted. I think the publisher saw that my body of work had been building toward this. Also, I grew up three hours away from Tulsa, and in that region there are a lot of the same stories about black communities being driven out of town after lynchings or violence—including, as I said, in my hometown.

I felt a connection to the story from growing up in this region. I was upset at not being taught all of these things that happened right around me. One thing I mentioned in the book, which is titled *Black Birds in the Sky*, is the Trail of Tears, the forced displacement of Native Nations from their ancestral homelands. The Trail of Tears came right through Springfield, and there were never any lessons on it.

I was able to turn some of that anger I have for the failings of the U.S. education system into passion for the book; I wanted to make sure that younger folks today don't feel the way I felt growing up. At the same time I want to be able to tell them this history in a way that's interesting to them—not like another textbook that is just a bunch of facts and no context.

I always want to make sure there's a story there, even in my non-fiction. I want to present it in a way that is interesting and conversational, but still respects the reader's intelligence. It's all a really delicate balance. I feel like every artist has that struggle or that challenge if they're trying to say something with their work. Setting out with the intention of tackling social justice through my art brings on a whole new set of challenges.

It's embarrassing to say now, but when I was a teenager, growing up in an apolitical town in the Midwest, I didn't even realize there were still protests going on. I thought that all stopped in the 1960s. At the same time, as much as I appreciate that protests are an effective way to engender change, I've always felt that my writing was the best way to use my voice.

I think that everyone just needs to find their specific skill and try to hone that, maybe even try out a few different types of things to find out the best way to engage in activism. Some people prefer protests, some are better at writing or activism through other forms of art, some call their congressional representatives to express the need for change. Just pay attention to what people are doing, and you can find ways to help.

I have this art print that hangs in my home, and I love it. It says, "Ask more questions." So that has become my motto, in both my work and personal life: "Ask more questions." It makes people uncomfortable a lot of times, but I think that's the real root of starting to change things, and maybe even finding out where you can best use your voice.

FOR MORE INFORMATION:
brandycolbert.com
Brandy Colbert's books:
   Pointe, 2014
   Little & Lion, 2017
   Finding Yvonne, 2018
   The Revolution of Birdie Randolph, 2019
   The Only Black Girls in Town, 2020
   The Voting Booth, 2020
   Black Birds in the Sky, 2021

'Knock on Every Door'

NADA AL-HANOOTI, 31, *is a Palestinian American community organizer. The daughter of immigrant parents, she is the executive director for the Michigan chapter of Emgage, an organization whose mission is to provide Muslim American communities with the framework and resources necessary to be politically engaged in America. Formerly, Nada served as a field coordinator for Rashida Tlaib for State Representative in Detroit and was responsible for organizing events and door-to-door initiatives as well as recruiting and managing volunteers.*

WHILE CANVASSING, I WAS literally seeing kids in the street selling drugs. I saw people live without electricity, with no water. I can't tell you how many times we heard gunshots while canvassing on the east side of Detroit. We saw a lot of homelessness, people squatting in abandoned houses. And, for me, growing up comfortably in Dearborn, that was a huge shock. "Oh my God, there are people that really live like this." And you begin to develop empathy for them. I was twenty years old. And that was the most memorable summer of my life.

When people are selling drugs, they're doing that as a last possible option to feed their families. And instead of blaming them for doing what they need to do to survive, Instead of criminalizing them, we need to recognize we have failed them. The system has failed them.

I'm Palestinian American. We were born to fight for the self-determination of our people. I remember my mom taking me to protests when I was five. That was normal within the Palestinian community, especially in my family, which was very politically active. That was when I first learned that human beings were being oppressed by other human beings. And that's where I started becoming angry—because of all the injustice people were suffering.

I always knew I wanted to get involved in politics, because I always knew I wanted to change the world in some capacity. I just didn't know how. So I went to college, where I majored in Political Science and Journalism, and minored in Women's Studies. First I thought I wanted to be a human rights lawyer. And then I'm like, *No, I'll just go into public policy.* Then it was, *I can't understand human rights without looking through an intersectional feminist lens.* I'm a Muslim, Arab, Palestinian woman. My intersections are constantly working against me, even in this realm of politics.

While an undergrad, I interned for Rashida Tlaib, who is a Congressperson now, but at that time was a state representative. That was my first hands-on experience of politics. I was very fortunate to be mentored by her, because unlike most politicians, she does the groundwork one-on-one with every community member. She knocks on every door. If the electricity's out from DTE Energy, she helps them get it back on. If they have no water, even if their house has bed bugs, she'll find a way to clean it out for them. She helped the most marginalized. And for me, it was: *This is what service is about.*

That's how I learned to be a good leader. This was true even in the way she treated the staff. She was always very kind to us. She was, "Well, if you finish this amount of doors and you do this, I'm going to give you my credit card. You can go get your nails done." Just that self-care and that love really uplifted us. And that's how we should do politics the right way.

Canvassing is form of activism. For me, it's the strongest form of activism. Activism is not only going to protest. I think protests are very performative. For me, it's about building something sustainable. If you're going to attend a protest, I want you to follow up and call your legislator and make sure you hold them accountable.

If you're protesting for Black Lives Matter, please call your legislator and have them sign on to the John Lewis Voting Rights Act or register people to vote. Enfranchising people is the most powerful thing you can do for them. Activism for me is when you canvas every single door, listen to their grievances, and make policy and advocate on behalf of them and bring them into the room.

Every time we have a meeting with a legislator, we are bringing in those people that are closest to the pain. For example, when we had legislative meetings about Kashmir, we had community members who have family there who don't have access to them. It's that cliche of really putting people above politics. So whatever we do, whether it's our lobby work or anything else, there's always people closest to the pain in the room. They need to speak for themselves to the legislator. We're here to change hearts and minds, and that's the way you do it.

As our organization's name suggests, we try to engage with and empower the Muslim community politically. The way we operate with our canvassers is we're trying to build leadership. So we call them "organizers." We pay them fifteen dollars an hour, because we believe in the minimum wage. And honestly, we live in a community where it's working class, and volunteering is a luxury.

We do a lot of storytelling. When I bring in my organizers, I say, "We're not here just making calls and trying to get Rashida to win. I know you're here, not because of Rashida, but because she represents something. You all have a stake in this. I want to hear your stories." So they talk about their family members getting deported. Or sometimes it's just like they want justice for Breonna Taylor.

For me, it's my Palestinian grandmother who I'm fighting for. She was born in a free Palestine. She died with her country being under occupation. It's about fighting the injustice of the past and for the freedom for the future for all the oppressed people.

It's so important to invest in the youth and let them know how important their voices are. As we speak, we're giving public comment to the redistricting commission in Michigan. We drew some maps. So I say to the young people, "We need you to make sure that our communities are represented." Again, it's about reminding them they have a personal stake, reminding them what they're truly fighting for.

As cheesy as it sounds, I ask myself what kind of world do I want to live in. The world I want to live in is a world where everyone truly loves and respects each other and uplifts each other. And so those are the values I bring to my team. We support each other when somebody needs help. If there is an issue with someone, you call them in out of love, not out. Calling them out is humiliating; calling them in is really a form of love and respect. Our Emgage community is growing, and it's so important to set your intention and set your values. And when you are authentic, it will resonate and it will be sustained.

Our organizers are all young. The oldest is twenty-seven. The youngest is fourteen and participates with his parents' permission, of course. They recruit others to canvas. We call that the "snowflake model." I tell them: "You are in charge of those volunteers. You have to take care of them, make sure they have all the resources." So that's how we build leadership. That's why I am intentional about empowering them, building leadership and giving them that responsibility.

Being happy is a form of social justice. It's a form of fighting back. So I always remind them, "I want you to take care of yourselves. I want you to be happy." I talk about mental health to them. "If you need to seek therapy, being happy is one way to stick it to our oppressors." So I teach that, too.

I ran for a seat on the Dearborn City Council in 2017 and lost. I'm asked a lot if I want to run for political office again. No, because honestly, people and PACs try to control you, and I don't like that. Also, I see a lot of politicians that are away from their family, and I have different values than that. I feel like activism starts within your family. You need to make sure they're prioritized the most.

But I think the biggest reason why I would never want to run for office again is because I really feel like I have more influence here in the background when I'm calling up the legislators and saying, "We need to have a meeting; you're messing up." When I'm registering people to vote, when I'm creating this whole new generation of leaders, it's more impactful than when this organization or this company is controlling you. I don't want to deal with that. In politics it's really hard to stay true to your values, but I think in this position I can.

I believe policy starts at the doors. If you're not learning the narratives of the most marginalized and you're not advocating through it in policy or creating policy through that, you're not doing the right work.

I think academia is extremely important. Read Malcolm X, read all these important people, read Kimberle Crenshaw, read slave narratives of female slaves. Everything. It's so important to know the history of that.

When I learned the history of these beautiful black women organizing for anti-lynching, I said, "Oh my God, why aren't they better known and celebrated?" MLK is great. All these civil rights heroes are great, but we have so many incredible women that are not talked about. And we really need to uplift them, which is why I deliberately uplift my grandmother. I want these stories to be heard.

It's really important to know how the movement started, where our struggles came from. Everything's interconnected. Read, know your history, know this history of all the most oppressed, know the history of the movement.

And again, you have to get on the ground. If you are not on the ground, you are not doing a good job representing us, because you do not know our pain. You're just speaking on our behalf because you read an article somewhere. That's not good enough for us.

When I finished grad school, I thought, *Okay, I know how to work with minority communities.* I remember one of my first events I did for Emgage. I went to the Yemeni community. We did a voting rights event and I had a panel. None of them were from the Yemeni community. I'm not from the Yemeni community. And I realized, *Oh my God, I literally came in as a colonizer telling these people like I know what's best for you and not even having any representation.*

So it's one thing to really read and agree what you're being taught academically, but racism and all this colonialism is really ingrained in your bodies, in ourselves. It takes a lot of work to undo it. That's why I preach to everyone, "Before you change your world, change yourself."

I read books, I've talked to a lot of people, I've challenged myself. And honestly, I preach mental health and therapy. I have a wonderful therapist, and we work through the immigration issues and through the trauma of the Palestine exodus and how it really still affects me to this day more than I ever thought it did.

One final piece of advice: please don't change your name; stay honest to who you are. We have capitulated enough. We are done compromising. Your name is just as American as everyone else's. You have a right to be here. If they're not making room at the table for you, squeeze yourself in no matter what.

FOR MORE INFORMATION:

https://emgageusa.org/emgage-michigan/

'Through Politics and Government'

MICHAEL STRAUTMANIS, *53, is executive vice president for external affairs at the Barack Obama Foundation in Chicago. His positions over the last fifteen years have included: vice president, citizenship, strategic programs at the Walt Disney Company; White House counselor to President Obama for strategic engagement; and chief of staff to White House Senior Advisor Valerie Jarrett.*

WHEN I WAS IN law school at the University of Illinois in the early 1990s, I started to get a sense that I had more to give, and I had more responsibility to give. There were issues around black student participation, black student enrollment, and the relationship that the university had with the community. There was going to be a sit-in at the home or office of the university president, and I went to the meeting to discuss it.

And we were in this meeting and I realized: *We're going to need lawyers, or at least somebody who has some sense of what's going on.* So a couple of friends and I decided we'd do the research and figure out what the rules were. If people got arrested, we'd get them the resources to get them out. And that was really the first time I ever got involved in activism.

I was raised by two educators. My mother was black, and my step-father was white. We lived in an immigrant neighborhood in Chicago, but my parents felt it was important for me to be steeped in black identity and the history of the civil rights movement. They didn't want me to accept negative stereotypes of black people. They wanted me to be prideful, to feel like I could achieve. So they infused these stories in me to inoculate me against the world.

At a young age I began seeing the world around me and realizing how much of a segregated city Chicago was. Visiting my family and my cousins on the South Side, I realized they were in the middle of a set of different circumstances than I was. We all had smart mouths and got in trouble. But the consequences for them had the potential to be much worse because of the police presence and attitudes where they lived. It started to feel unfair to me.

In grade school, I was in trouble a lot. During in-school detention a black teacher would sit with me and play filmstrips of the movement—of the march across the Edmund Pettus Bridge, of Dr. King. I got into some trouble in high school, too. I read it now that there were expectations of me that I was not meeting—and, given our history, they wanted me to know why it was important for me to step up and step forward.

I was in high school in 1983 when Harold Washington was elected Chicago's first black mayor. My parents were both engaged in politics and supported him, and I was excited when he won. Seeing what he faced from the innuendos of the white Republican candidate he ran against and the barriers put up by powerful white aldermen who wanted to control things started to explain to me some of the inequities in our city and country.

My interest in politics continued beyond high school. In college and law school, I got involved in presidential campaigns and Carol Moseley Braun's successful run for the Senate in 1992, when she became the first black female U.S. Senator. After law school I moved to Oak Park, a suburb immediately west of Chicago, and became a precinct captain for the Oak Park Democratic Party.

In going door to door, getting people out to vote and hearing about their concerns, I started to understand how relevant government was to the lives of everyday people, and, frankly, how disconnected it was. This realization is what really started me on the path to activism through politics and organizing.

At the same time, being aware that I'd survived as a kid even though I'd come very close to getting into serious trouble and at times had had problematic relationships with my parents, I started thinking about kids on the other side of that thin line. Having had an absent birth father myself, my heart had always gone out to kids in the foster care system. I'd always felt like I wanted to give some support and inspiration.

The law firm I was going to work for allowed incoming associates to do pro bono volunteer work while preparing for the bar exam. I spent two months in the Cook County Public Guardian's office, where my eyes were opened to the abuse and neglect in our foster care system. And then my friend Nigel Tillman suggested I join the board of Jamal Place, a local boys' home.

At Jamal Place, I met people who were like living saints, completely dedicated to uplifting the lives of others. Again, I had this sense that there were things that I could do with my own presence, being a young black man who could relate to and speak to and engage with these young people. Seeing how little we were accomplishing in a systemic way made me think, *there's got to be another way for me to get at this and make a difference*. But at the time it was my side gig, a volunteer thing. I was going to be a big-time lawyer.

In the end I saw that the best way for me to make a difference was through politics and government. I just kept volunteering. I organized young lawyers to be poll workers, got involved in campaigns like Barack Obama's run for the Illinois State Senate in 1996. That same year I helped out in the Clinton-Gore reelection campaign. I just realized that I was good at this—good at organizing people, at public speaking.

I could understand the issues I cared about like poverty and education and could see they weren't changing—that there was a political dialogue that was kind of irrelevant to the issues and things that I cared about. But I also saw that Barack and others were being successful in driving a different dialogue and talking about different issues and then getting elected and having the ability to put their agendas in place.

Of course the culmination of this was when Barack was elected president in 2008. I became chief of staff to Valerie Jarrett, who was his senior advisor. Then after two years in that position, I spent three years as a counselor for strategic engagement. Now post-presidency, I'm executive vice president for external affairs for the Obama Foundation in Chicago.

But before all of that, I went to Washington. After the '96 election, I ended up talking my way into a job in the Clinton administration at the U.S. Agency for International Development. That led to two transformative months in Kosovo, where I saw the tremendous impact our country can make around the world. After that I also worked on the John Kerry presidential campaign. I also worked on issues with the Congressional Black Caucus, and I started thinking I could really make a difference in the world doing this.

As a staff person or aide, you're there at the service of the member. I keep telling aides, "Nobody elected us to anything. It's not *our* issues." They have to be the issues that the person that you're working with and for cares about. At the same time there's an opportunity to move the needle.

Activism is about passion, it's about shaking people out of their day-to-day and getting them to join. There's gotta be a spark, a moment of inspiration. So if you are going to join a staff or work as an aide, the first thing I would ask is: "Are you moved by what it is that they're doing or what it is that they're saying?"

Number two: "Do you see a track record of people on staff being able to get opportunity?" Some places are just deeply hierarchical. You could work there forever and you'll never get a shot. That's cool if you just want to be a cog in the machine. But If you are going to want to grow, to have more influence and more change, look at the track record of others.

Finally, and I cannot stress this enough: you have to choose an area in which you are going to become an expert, an area in which you're going to go deep. Too many young people, including myself when I was young, want to be involved in a bunch of things, which means they're generalists. You have to pick an area. For me, it was law, which turned into civil rights law, which turned into a role as a legislative director. And then from that, I had the opportunity to be chief counsel. And then I got a chance to build out from there.

I actually think the experience that has made me the most effective in organizing change is my time in theatre. I was a kid that was in all the plays, had all the leads my senior year in high school, even went to college as a Theatre major. I still try to do it when I get a chance.

Theatre is about listening. I think I'm the most fully-myself when I am all in listening to somebody else's story. One of the greatest gifts you can give to another human being is to listen to their story. It's incredibly empowering if, through someone's story, you can give them a path to make the change that they want to see. You can give people the path to being a part of something else, something bigger than themselves. That remains the most powerful thing in the world.

if you want to move policy, you gotta find a way to get people who have literally no idea what you're talking about to care. You do that through storytelling because a powerful story will resonate with you, and you'll be able to see yourself in it because of your own experiences.

For example, seeing yourself as a parent who worries about your child and wants what's best for your child. The connection there with Senator Obama and President Obama was obvious, right? He grew up without a father. He was a man who was working really hard to be the best father he could. He saw young people without that guidance to be a parent, and he wanted to find a way to help and support them, knowing that in doing so he would make all of our lives richer and better, not just theirs. So that story, I think, is the through-line.

I always say as an activist, as a changemaker, if you can't tell that story, you shouldn't move forward with the issue. Just keep working on it, keep talking to people, keep listening, keep learning, keep figuring it out until there is a story that moves somebody who is not involved in the day-to-day and not personally impacted in a visceral way by the issue that you care about. I see many activists throwing themselves against the wall, constantly not making any progress because they can't get anyone outside of their own circle to get connected to the issue that they care about.

Find the story.

FOR MORE INFORMATION:

Obama.org

'We Directly Invest'

DON KATZ, 70, is the founder and executive chairman of Audible, Inc., the leading creator and provider of premium audio storytelling. Prior to starting the company in 1995, Katz was a globetrotting, award-winning journalist and author. Audible is widely considered one of the most socially responsible "corporate citizens" in the country, and Katz has been recognized by Living Cities as one of America's "Top 25 Disruptive Leaders" for his work on behalf of urban transformation in Newark, where Audible is headquartered.

I WAS POLITICIZED AND, in many ways, radicalized by the character of my upbringing and by my understanding of history and the times in which I came of age. I knew there were profound moral underpinnings to my father's sense of patriotism when he chose to take huge personal risks to enlist in World War II—running away from home at seventeen and ending up becoming a scout behind enemy lines. He was a highly decorated hero fighting murderous fascism in Europe. So I had that as grounding.

As my own perceptions of social and personal purpose evolved, the inequities of society as evidenced by Chicago in the 1960s became more and more apparent. I saw this firsthand in high school, when I was tutoring kids in the Cabrini-Green Homes on the North Side, seeing how the warehousing of poor people by government was dehumanizing and fundamentally born out of fear and racism.

I was one of those suburban kids of my times who saw himself as part of the resistance, far to the left of his more traditionally liberal parents. In 1967, at fifteen, I was going to the South Side and saw Fred Hampton up close at a Black Panther breakfast. I was tear-gassed and chased while protesting the trial of the Chicago 7. During my early childhood, I was aware that black people still couldn't vote in parts of the country, and I took to heart and protested what happened to people like Hampton and the Freedom Riders down south.

In college at NYU, I became immersed in the literature of people like James Baldwin and Ralph Ellison. After being fortunate enough to have an amazing tutelage by Ellison, a professor at NYU, I went to England for graduate school to study politics, economics, and international relations. I thought I might be a speechwriter, like a Ted Sorensen, who actually had power in the Kennedy Administration. I think I was interested in that because I couldn't see myself being published in any of the more serious-minded journals of progressive thinking, where you went deep and tried to tell the truth almost as if it were a story with a beginning, middle, and end.

And then, while in London, at age twenty-three, I got an assignment from *Rolling Stone*. I covered the death of Francisco Franco from the perspective of the Basque ETA underground, trying to make people aware that fascism was still alive and well in Europe and that the underground, which had been characterized as terrorists, actually had a nationalist cause that owned a level historical and moral integrity.

From that point, I went from one long story to another for the magazine as a London-based contributing editor. I went to Italy and wrote about the Red Brigade. I went to Ethiopia. You want to talk about being an activist! You can organize or write about it all you want, the revolutionaries I was seeking out were literally willing to be killed, to blow themselves up, or in some cases kill for a cause. I was just fascinated by this dark and complicated world of geopolitics. I did a *Rolling Stone* cover story on the occasion of Jane Fonda's fortieth birthday, and there I highlighted her activism and then-underappreciated role in ending the Vietnam War as opposed to her celebrity alone. .

I was always looking to make an impact through the power of storytelling, to allow people to hold a mirror up and see themselves in the context of historical events. It wasn't the same as becoming a full-time activist on the ground, but it was a way of trying to express a sense of differentiated ethics and ideas.

> *After some twenty years of writing articles, essays, and books that provided new perspectives to events transpiring everywhere from war zones to board rooms to family homes, Katz had the inspiration for Audible. A decade later, in 2007, he moved the company head-quarters from suburban Wayne, NJ, to what some might say was a forgotten and foreboding city—Newark. Consultants told him he would lose 25 percent of his workforce; he lost none.*

I wanted to have the adventure of starting this company, which I believed could have a massive cultural impact. The world of vernacular storytelling should have been a primary art in this country, but wasn't. There was a structurally missing piece to the American media landscape. Having been Ralph Ellison's tutee and taken his course called "American Vernacular," I understood that American literature at its best was a function of how we spoke, how we told stories around campfires—how we bragged, consoled, lamented and felt.

I had a pretty significant view on how business and economics worked because I had written about the subject as a journalist, including writing two books about Sears and Nike that took nine years of reporting. I knew that if you could use these new technology networks to deliver profound experiences of words, performed with skill and nuance, you could change the lives of the primary creators, performers, and listeners. It also seemed to be an amazing opportunity for me to be less of a lone wolf than I was as a professional writer, to have colleagues, and to use some of my persuasive skills that I'd employed to get people to tell me the truth when they often didn't tell it to others.

As soon as Audible began to turn the corner and achieve success, I wanted to figure out how the company could make a societal difference, but in a way that could promote potential alternative models for so-cial amelioration and equality-making in counterpoint to what was not working in a city like Newark despite an elaborate philanthropic sector. As our company "People Principles" explain it: "We strive to make a positive impact on the cities we call home because we believe companies can have hearts and souls and missions that transcend financial success."

Once we moved to Newark, we began to do things designed to get closer to the root of some of the problems. We started something as simple as paying all our employees five hundred dollars a month after taxes to move to Newark and be part of the city's comeback, and then we would measure the small business and job impact of the spending our people reinjected into Newark. Since then we've put about half a billion dollars into Newark and generated about twice that amount in economic activity.

We also said there would be no more nepotistic internships of privi-leged friends. You had to be a kid from Newark Public Schools to be an intern. And internships would be paid; no free internships. The city has some terrific public charter schools and public magnets, with which I have been involved since long before we moved into the city, and we began drawing these wonderful kids who had such energy.

If you look at the last thirty or forty years, the more typical model for corporate involvement was almost haphazardly giving money to charity. I knew that in the past all three sectors capable of generat-ing and injecting money and policy into society to provide for the common welfare—the government, the philanthropic sector and the private sector—had been too often running on auto-pilot, in particular as regards the absence of wealth as the source of so much unconscionable inequality in disenfranchised cities. We decided to be a company that, by its stated precepts, is committed to pursuing ways to redress inequality.

To do that we directly invest; we don't do arms-length philanthropy. Philanthropy is too often giving away money by people who have earned returns through intensive and creative use of inputs and measurable outputs, and they don't apply rigor to their giving. A glance again at our "People Principles" indicates we are in Newark, and we understand that you have to make distributable wealth in the more marginalized locations; it's not a trickle-down process. You have to do it program-matically. We would look at what Barcelona and Berlin were doing to discern more positively disruptive models for equitable turnarounds while so many decision-makers rarely sought best practices.

As example, we started Newark Venture Partners (NVP) to plant little "Audibles" in Newark, because there is academic research that shows that a high-tech job generates five jobs at different levels, whereas a manufacturing job has minimal incremental job rub-off. I realized I couldn't hire all of the amazing talent being created by groundbreaking new ways of teaching in Newark myself and needed an ecosystem of cooler companies to do that. The older thinking, the liberal thinking, has been to airlift the kids out of the urban corridor, but if you do that, they often don't return after college because of their inability to envisage their home town as a place with jobs and entrepreneurial opportunities where they can make a difference.

One example of a win from the Newark Venture Partners Labs, an early stage tech company incubator, which nurtures companies in downtown Newark, is 1Huddle, which markets an app that gamifies workforce training. It's grown to forty employees worldwide, half of whom work in Newark, and it now supports Newark by offering training to not-for-profits and city residents and is actively recruiting Newark-born and -educated talent to come back and join in urban renaissance.

When COVID hit, our crisis response was a start-up called Newark Working Kitchens. From long experience of the philanthropic status quo, I knew the kneejerk reaction to food disruptions was going to be food pantry donations and food lines. But there were a lot of things that made this problematic in historically injured urban core environ-ments. People, especially in senior or disabled housing, didn't have cars in poor cities to get to the food. Co-morbidity and COVID infections levels worked against leaving home.

Small largely nonwhite-owned food businesses were dying at higher rates and few of them had accountants or lawyers helping get government assistance. Newark Working Kitchens would instead go to a Newark restaurant and say: "We'll buy two hundred meals a day from you at ten dollar a piece. In return, stay open and keep your employees. We will use our Audible vans and the company food budget we're not using—because we closed our cafeteria—and we will deliver meals in a targeted way to the people who need it, including the homeless." So far, through this form of activated giving, we've served almost 1.4 million meals through almost forty local restaurants, sustaining hundreds of jobs.

Another program, Audible Scholars, grew out of our research showing many of the amazing kids coming out of the schools we work with and our internship program weren't finishing college. They were placed in virtually lily-white schools and, despite financial packages, had a hard time affording school. So now our Audible Scholars get a monthly stipend and the opportunity to work full-time at Audible during breaks. Some return as full-time employees after college, rejoining the city's renaissance. The disparities between standing wealth in the white part of New Jersey and the state's largest cities, filled with black, Latino, and immigrant populations, is just unacceptable.

Not everything we have tried to do in the spirit of finding scalable new models to address urban inequality has worked, and COVID really hurt, but I continue to tell other corporate leaders that much of what we try to do is good for business. If you look at research on brand affinity and social purpose, younger people don't want to shop at a company that they don't think as having a societal perspective beyond money. Younger employs tend to want to work for a company possessed of an ethical lens beyond status quo giving.

It's not risk-your-life-for-a-cause activism as I observed up close during my writing years, but I hope it's work worthy of consideration.

FOR MORE INFORMATION:

https://www.audible.com/about/people-principles
https://about.audible.com/impact
https://www.donald-katz.com/
The Big Store: Inside the Crisis and Revolution at Sears (1987)
Home Fires: An Intimate Portrait of One Middle-Class Family in Postwar America (1992)
Just Do It: The Nike Spirit in the Corporate World (1994)
The King of the Ferret Leggers and Other True Stories (2001)
The Valley of the Fallen: And Other Places (2001)

Index